When
FOOTBALL *Was*
FOOTBALL

CHARLTON ATHLETIC

© Haynes Publishing, 2014

The right of Michael Walsh to be identified as the author of this Work has been asserted
by him in accordance with the Copyright, Designs & Patents Act 1988.

All rights reserved. No part of this publication may be reproduced, stored in a retrieval system
or transmitted, in any form or by any means, electronic, mechanical, photocopying, recording
or otherwise, without prior permission in writing from the publisher.

First published in 2014

A catalogue record for this book is available from the British Library

ISBN: 978-0-85733-714-6

Published by Haynes Publishing, Sparkford, Yeovil,
Somerset BA22 7JJ, UK
Tel: 01963 442030 Fax: 01963 440001
Int. tel: +44 1963 442030 Int. fax: +44 1963 440001
E-mail: sales@haynes.co.uk
Website: www.haynes.co.uk

Haynes North America Inc., 861 Lawrence Drive,
Newbury Park, California 91320, USA

Images © Mirrorpix

Creative Director: Kevin Gardner
Designed for Haynes by BrainWave

Printed and bound in the US

When
FOOTBALL *Was*
FOOTBALL

CHARLTON ATHLETIC

A Nostalgic Look at a Century of the Club

Michael Walsh

Contents

Introduction

The 1998 Division One play-off final, arguably the most thrilling match staged beneath the old twin towers. Charlton goalkeeper Saša Ilić – now a juice therapist in Montenegro – is buried by Steve Brown, Eddie Youds, Steve Jones, Mark Bowen and Shaun Newton on a nerve-shredding afternoon against Sunderland that no Addick will ever forget.

But then there have been a few of those down the years. It's the memories, the legends, the heroes that keep you going back – that offer hope and solace in the darkest hours (or years at Selhurst Park). The greatest days of your life? Your first-born, and being one of the 33,000 Charlton Athletic fans at Wembley to see Saša save that penalty on 25th May 1998. Not necessarily in that order . . .

Foreword

I signed professional forms for Charlton Athletic in July 1962 and am still a part of this very special football club more than 50 years later. These photographs go back even further than me, and are a wonderful journey down memory lane. Sometimes painful, occasionally glorious . . . never dull!

I look at 'Sailor' Brown, shorts held up with string after being washed so many times that the elastic's gone, and I realize how times had changed even when I started out.

I gave up A-levels and had to tell my headmaster I was leaving to become a professional footballer. "A footballer!" he exploded. "What a waste of a good education."

Lenny Glover was signed around the same time and we were getting £7 a week. Lenny had earned double that as a Covent Garden barrow boy. He became English football's most expensive winger when Charlton sold him to Leicester in 1967.

Before leaving school that summer of '62 I turned out for the end-of-term match between pupils and staff. Five weeks later I was playing for Charlton in front of nearly 40,000 at Roker Park against Charlie Hurley and Brian Clough.

My family were all mad Newcastle fans, and I was brought up to follow them. But through these pictures I am almost reliving the moment that all changed. It was the last game of the 1957–58 season and my local club Charlton needed a draw against Blackburn to return to the First Division after relegation the year before. They lost 4-3. I was one of nearly 60,000 people at The Valley that day and I'll never forget the silence afterwards, like mourners at a funeral. That's when Charlton Athletic became my team.

So I was awestruck as a 15-year-old when I was invited to play a trial match at that great bowl of The Valley, home to so many of my heroes, vividly recalled here – Sam Bartram, Don Welsh, Johnny Summers, Stuart Leary.

Another Charlton legend leaps from the pages. We were training one day and I recall asking who the stranger was in the tight blue top, which was a cut above our old kit. "That's Eddie Firmani," I was told. "He's over visiting from Italy."

Of course Eddie came back and ended up as my team-mate and manager. In fact, the only thing that did seem to change in my 17 happy years as a player at The Valley was the manager. Although, as you can see, we led the revolution in football shirts back in the Swinging Sixties!

This book is a fitting tribute to the many great players and fans who make Charlton Athletic such a special football club.

Keith Peacock

FOOTBALL –STATS–

Keith Peacock

Name: Keith Peacock

Born: Barnehurst, Kent, 2nd May 1945

Position: Inside-forward

Charlton career: 1962–79

Appearances: 567

Goals: 107

He was the first Football League substitute, but is celebrated at Charlton as a magnificent one-club man, making more outfield appearances than any other player.

Take Courage

Opening Shots
1905-1932

Step back in time to 1906. Edwardian England was casting off its crinolines and corsets, and the nation was enthralled by a runaway bestseller foretelling German beastliness, entitled *The Invasion of 1910*.

On a sunny May afternoon, a *Daily Mirror* snapper joined the lethal ladies from Charlton and Kidbrooke Rifle Club at their firing range in a blot on the landscape known as the Charlton Sandpits.

"Women Ready for the Invasion of 1910 or Any Other Time", declared the headline over these intriguing views of what would later become The Valley.

Charlton Athletic were born the previous year, a mile or so up-river from the big guns of Woolwich Arsenal, who had been a Football League team since 1893 and were playing in front of 20,000-plus crowds in Division One. But the Arsenal – pictured at their Manor Ground in Plumstead in 1906 – decamped to North London in 1913 after a mind-boggling planned amalgamation with Fulham at Craven Cottage had been outlawed by the League.

It left the football field clear for Charlton to emerge as South London's finest.

The Boys of 1906

RIGHT: The founding sons of Charlton Athletic kitted out for their debut season of local football, possibly with a minder or three for those first tussles with Millwall.

And How They Grew Up . . .

1921 Join Football League Division Three (South) after a season in the Southern League. **1929** Promoted as Division Three (South) Champions. **1933** Bottom of Division Two and relegated. **1935** Promoted as Division Three (South) Champions again. **1936** Promoted as Division Two runners-up. **1937** Football League Championship runners-up. **1946** Losing FA Cup finalists. **1947** FA Cup winners. **1957** Relegated to Division Two. **1972** Relegated to Division Three. **1975** Promoted to Division Two. **1980** Relegated to Division Three. **1981** Promoted to Division Two. **1986** Promoted to Division One (the proper one). **1987** Stay up through Division One relegation play-offs. **1990** Relegated to Division Two. **1996** Stay down after play-off semi-final defeat to Crystal Palace. **1998** Promoted to Premier League after play-offs. **1999** Relegated to Football League Division One. **2000** Promoted to Premier League as Football League Champions. **2007** Relegated to the Championship. **2009** Relegated to League One. **2010** Stay down after League One semi-final play-off defeat to Swindon. **2012** Promoted as League One Champions.

Before They Were Famous . . .

9th June 1905 Charlton Athletic founded by football-loving teenagers from the back-to-backs huddled beside the Thames between Woolwich and Greenwich. Their first ground is Siemens Meadow, a glorified refuse tip. **22nd December 1906** Join Lewisham Junior League's Division Three, kicking-off with a 4-0 win over Braby Ironworks. **2nd March 1907** Millwall Rangers are thumped 7-1 and Charlton celebrate their first League title without losing a match. **17th April 1908** Charlton player Bill Pirie (pictured) is drowned in a rowing tragedy on the Thames. **31st October 1908** Charlton christened 'The Haddocks' in a local newspaper cartoon. **1919** After years of ground-hopping, a new home is carved out of Charlton Sandpits, otherwise known as 'The Swamps', with its flooded excavations. **13th September 1919** The pools have been filled in, a pitch flattened out with a borrowed steam-roller and The Valley hosts its first match – a 2-0 win over Summerstown in the Southern Suburban League. **6th March 1920** Tottenham Hotspur reserves play a friendly at The Valley and are winning 3-0 when the game is abandoned in a monsoon. One of the Spurs scorers is a young Jimmy Seed. **Summer 1920** Charlton turn professional and join the Southern League. Their first manager is Walter Rayner, an ex-player who coached at Tottenham and Arsenal. **27th August 1921** The first Football League match at The Valley. 13,000 see Charlton beat Exeter 1-0 in Division Three (South).

Looking down on the wide open space of Siemens Meadow that became Charlton's first home in 1905. Just downstream from historic Greenwich, the anonymous Thames backwater of Charlton had its share of dramas before League football's soap opera arrived. The sinking of a tramp steamer after colliding with the liner *Corinthian* made front-page news in June 1913 (right). Charlton's away fixture at Wealdstone in the London League that October merited the briefest mention. Six years later a 6-2 reverse away to Ilford was duly recorded in the fine print on the *Daily Mirror* sports pages (left).

The great hulk of HMS *Warspite*, an old ship of the line turned into a naval training vessel, was a stirring landmark on the Thames at Charlton until the turn of the 20th century – a time when boys' imaginations were being fired by Association Football as well as heroic sea tales.

Charlton's fishy nickname has caused as much bewilderment as any dodgy refereeing decision over the years. Club historians credit it to the players' liking for fish and chip suppers after battering their opponents.

This tradition spawned a surreal cartoon series in the local newspaper, where the club was dubbed 'The Haddocks', which was translated into Sarf London-speak to become 'The Addicks'. The owner of the team's favourite chippy was reputed to show up for matches and parade around the ground with a fish nailed to a pole. Legend adds that whenever Charlton lost – a rare occurrence in those days – they would make do with a cheaper piece of cod.

Match-Fixer, War Hero, Charlton Legend . . .

Arthur Whalley was forbidden even to enter a football ground, let alone play in one, after being banned from the game for life over a notorious betting scandal. He was at Manchester United when he helped fix the result of a match against Liverpool on Good Friday 1915 – cashing in at 7-1 on a 2-0 United win. It was so blatant that fans howled in derision, especially when a Liverpool co-conspirator blazed a penalty wide. Whalley – who did not actually play in the game – won redemption in the trenches, being badly wounded at the Battle of Passchendaele in 1917. The slate was wiped clean after the First World War in recognition of his service to King and Country. After a spell at Southend, he arrived at The Valley in his mid-30s and was a linchpin of Charlton's first three seasons in League football, playing 88 matches, but he owes his Addicks legend status more perhaps to the greatest giant-killing run in FA Cup history.

Football's Forgotten Giantkillers

In just their second season as a Football League Division Three (South) side, Charlton defeated no fewer than three Division One aristocrats, all previous winners of the famous trophy.

The Addicks were given no hope after being drawn away at Manchester City in the first round. Arthur Whalley, the prodigal son of Manchester United, scored the deciding goal in a 2-1 victory. The *Daily Mirror* trumpeted "Charlton's Sensation", telling how "Manchester City, who have only lost once this season, succumbed to London's 'babes of the League' . . . Remarkable as it seems, the Charlton goalkeeper did not have a single shot to save in the first half."

Abraham 'Kosha' Goodman gave Charlton the lead after 42 minutes. City were back on terms three minutes after half-time and, according to the report, "the visiting combination was almost swamped" before Whalley headed the winner seven minutes from the end.

CHARLTON ATHLETIC man (centre) clearing from a North End partnership that looked a little dangerous. Charlton won 2—0.

West Bromwich (stripes) on the defensive against Charlton Athletic, who were the winners 1—nil, after a splendid game. West Bromwich goalie is seen fisting clear.

PRESTON player (white shirt) and a Charlton man in heads-up duel. The home team scored in the second half.

> *Charlton, by overthrowing Preston North End, made themselves the most talked about side in the country on Saturday. Wiseacres shook their head and whispered 'fluke' after the Valley side had overcome Manchester City in the first round, but the defeat of last year's finalists is a completely satisfying answer to such criticisms.*
>
> Daily Mirror

Charlton defeated Preston 2-0 in front of 22,490 at The Valley in the second round of the FA Cup. Kosha Goodman scored with a piledriver from 30 yards just after half-time before Steve Smith's strike despatched the 1922 beaten FA Cup finalists. Whalley was again man of the match. West Bromwich Albion were next up at The Valley in a game settled once more by Goodman. In front of 35,000 fans, he pounced on a rebound from a shot by one-eyed Charlton forward Bob Thomson to score the only goal. The minnows were drawn at home again in the quarter-finals, this time to Bolton, when more than 41,000 people were shoehorned into The Valley. Crush barriers collapsed, supporters were flung on to the pitch and children were carried away unconscious by rescuers, including Charlton manager, Walter Rayner. Bolton, packed full of internationals, won by the only goal of the game before going on to win the equally chaotic first Wembley FA Cup final. For Charlton, a remarkable Cup run brought fleeting fame – but the tens of thousands who had flocked to watch the team soon melted away like Thames mist.

CHARLTON ATHLETIC fail to score, as Pearson fists away for West Bromwich (stripes).

Wood punching clear for Charlton Athletic, who went down at home before Bolton Wanderers.

WEST BROMWICH ALBION goalkeeper, Pearson, saves against Charlton, who won by the only goal.

24th April 1923 Just six weeks after the Bolton disappointment the *Daily Mirror* reports that the "four clear goals defeat at Newport on Saturday was the biggest reverse Charlton have sustained this season. Further, Charlton have failed to gain a single point in Wales, for, besides the Newport defeat, they were beaten at Swansea, Aberdare and Merthyr." **10th May 1923** Wing-half Seth Plum becomes the first Charlton player to play for England, winning his one and only cap in a 4-1 victory against France at Stade Pershing, Paris. **December 1923** Charlton leave The Valley because of dwindling attendances and move in with non-League neighbours Catford. The *Mirror* reports: "The new Charlton ground at Catford can be reached by the Southern Railway, five tram services and 10 bus routes." It was certainly more convenient than what later Charlton followers could expect when the club ground-shared with Crystal Palace. **22nd December 1923** First match at Catford is a 0-0 draw with Northampton. The final indignity for fans is that the Addicks discard their traditional red and white and turn out in new light blue and dark blue colours. **3rd May 1924** Crowds slump to 1,000, the ill-judged Catford merger is abandoned and it's back to The Valley for Charlton. **1925-26** Charlton finish second bottom in the Football League and successfully apply for re-election. **4th May 1929** Charlton win 2-0 at Walsall to clinch their first promotion and the Division Three (South) Championship, pipping South London rivals Palace on goal average. Addicks manager Alex Macfarlane is too nervous to watch and paces the streets of Walsall for the entire game.

RIGHT: The *Mirror* records the final Division Three (South) table of 1928-29 with Charlton as champions – and covers the Catford move of a few years earlier.

FINAL LEAGUE PLACINGS

DIVISION III. (N.)				DIVISION III. (S.)			
Stockport . 3	Barrow .. 2			Walsall ... 0	Charlton .. 2		
Crewe A... 3	Wrexham . 1			Gillingham 1	Merthyr .. 0		
Bradford C 3	S. Shields. 1			Newport .. 2	Norwich .. 0		
Rotherham 5	Rochdale . 0			Bristol R.. 1	Coventry .. 1		
Southport. 2	Lincoln .. 1			Swindon .. 2	Exeter 0		
Tranmere.. 3	Chest'rfield 0			Plymouth . 2	B'nemouth . 0		
Wigan 1	N. Bri'ton. 1			Palace 1	Brighton .. 2		
Halifax ... 2	Doncaster.. 2			Q.P.R. 1	Luton 1		
Accrington 4	Nelson 4			Torquay .. 2	Southend .. 1		
				Fulham 1	Brentford.. 0		
				Watford ... 1	North'pton. 1		
	P.	W.	Pts.		P.	W.	Pts.
Bradford City	42	27	63	Charlton Athletic	42	23	54
Stockport County .	42	28	52	Crystal Palace ..	42	23	54
Wrexham	42	21	52	Northampton	42	20	52
Wigan Borough ...	42	21	51	Plymouth Argyle .	42	20	52
Doncaster R.	42	20	50	Fulham	42	21	52
Lincoln City	42	21	48	Q.P. Rangers	42	19	52
Tranmere Rovers .	42	22	47	Luton	42	19	49
Carlisle United ..	42	19	46	Watford	42	19	48
Crewe Alexandra .	42	18	44	Bournemouth	42	19	47
South Shields	42	18	44	Swindon	42	15	43
Chesterfield	42	18	41	Coventry City ...	42	14	42
Southport	42	16	40	Southend Utd. ...	42	15	41
Halifax	42	13	39	Brentford	42	14	38
New Brighton ...	42	15	39	Walsall	42	13	38
Nelson	42	13	39	Brighton	42	16	38
Rotherham Utd..	42	15	39	Newport County .	42	13	35
Rochdale	42	13	36	Norwich City ...	42	14	34
Accrington	42	13	34	Torquay Utd.	42	14	34
Darlington	42	13	33	Bristol Rovers ..	42	13	33
Barrow	42	10	28	Merthyr	42	11	30
Hartlepools Utd..	42	10	26	Exeter City	42	9	23
Ashington	42	8	23	Gillingham	42	10	20

Dancing on ice: Charlton, in white, slip and slide to a 2-1 win in an FA Cup second-round replay at snowbound Kettering on 15th December 1927. The replay fixture was held on a midweek afternoon, which was common right up until the early 1960s.

CHARLTON'S NEW GROUND.

Match with Northampton To Be Played at The Mount on Saturday.

The opening of the new Charlton Athletic ground at Catford on Saturday, with the visit of Northampton, will not be in any way an official opening, as the ground is not yet sufficiently finished.

It is expected, however, that an official opening will take place about the end of January. The object of playing at Catford as soon as possible is because of the poor support received at the Valley this season, where the gates have averaged less than 5,000.

Accommodation for about 15,000 will be available at Catford by Saturday, and when the ground is finished it will house 70,000 spectators in comfort. The new grand stand at Charlton will not be transported until the close season.

Travelling facilities to the new ground are very good.

HOME, SWEET HOME.

Charlton Athletic Decide to Forsake the Mount for the Valley.

The directors of the Charlton Athletic F.C. have decided to return to their old ground at Charlton next season.

The club removed to its new ground at Catford as recently as last Christmas, but the support received there was very meagre. A further expenditure of something like £12,000 would be required to finish the ground and erect a grand stand.

In such discouraging circumstances, the directors are not prepared to proceed.

The old supporters of the club at Charlton have invited the club to return and, after careful consideration, the directors have decided to do so.

Pictured left, Charlton's Dutch goalkeeper Gerard Keizer collects against Leeds United during a 1-0 defeat at The Valley on 24th October 1931. Closest to him is Norman Smith, a veteran of the club's earliest days in the Football League. Beyond are the still un-concreted sandy eastern slopes of The Valley bowl. Fathers attending matches were known to let their children venture off and play in the sandpits for the duration.

> *When the whistle was blown by referee Capt AJ Prince-Fox, hundreds of Charlton fans rushed on to the pitch. . . When the players finally reached Charlton Station, the neighbouring streets were impassable because of the throngs of fans.*
>
> The Daily Mirror on the promotion-clinching match at Walsall

Charlton Athletic at the end of the 1930–31 season, with five Scots and two Welshmen, including Dai Astley, who had been sold to Aston Villa for £2,750 by the time the new campaign kicked off. Astley later managed Inter Milan. Geordie defender Norman Smith's 449 appearances over 14 seasons at Charlton – including the Catford débâcle – is bettered only by Sam Bartram, Keith Peacock and John Hewie. Jack Pugsley was a Division Three (North) Champion with Grimsby before helping Charlton to the Division Three (South) Championship in 1928–29. Dai Astley, Norman Smith, Jack Horton, Albert Langford

and Harry Wyper were all survivors of that first promotion side. Skipper Bobby McKay had been a Football League Champion with Newcastle in 1927. Back row, left to right: John Pitcairn, trainer Mr Hopkins, Norman Smith, Peter Robertson, Albert Langford, Mr Dorward, Jack Pugsley. Front row: Harry Wyper, Bobby McKay, Dai Astley, Tom McLeod, Jack Horton, Tom Pritchard.

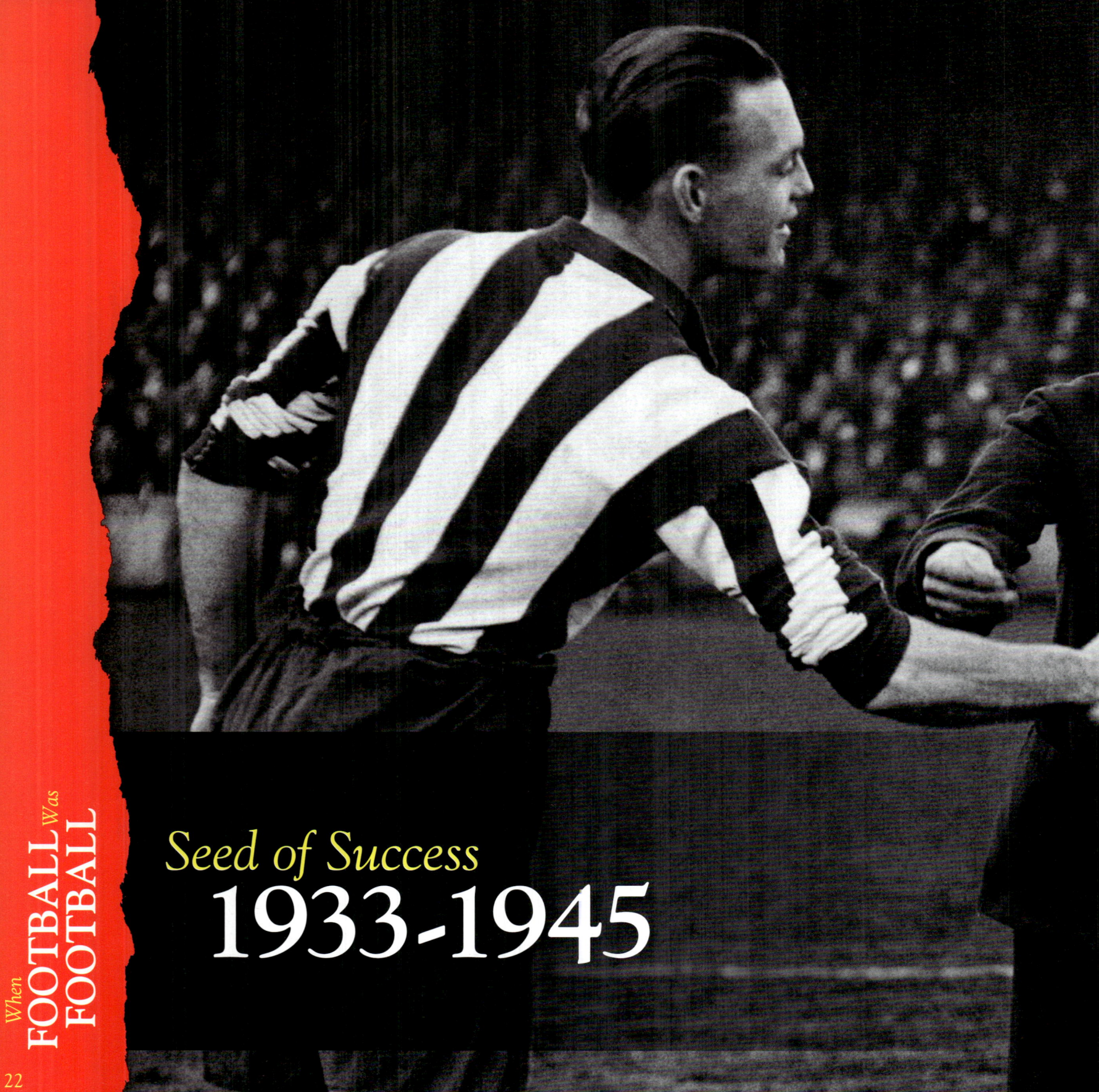

Seed of Success
1933-1945

> "Simply because a club has a great name and half a dozen stars on its books doesn't necessarily mean that they are a better team than we are.
>
> Jimmy Seed "

Jimmy Seed, seen here on the right representing Sheffield Wednesday, shakes hands with Reading captain Alf Messer before an FA Cup fourth-round match in January 1929. Reading won 1-0. Seed, an FA Cup winner with Spurs in 1921, had the consolation of leading Wednesday to the League title that season – and the one after. He was a fine footballer who would turn out to be a great manager.

Taste for Glory

Jimmy Seed was an FA Cup winner with Tottenham when they beat Wolves 1-0 at Stamford Bridge in 1921. The clipping below salutes Charlton on the brink of completing their rise to Division One – although the caption writer didn't know his Oakes from his Prior!

Prior   Oakes

ALL BUT IN DIVISION I

Only One Danger to Charlton

Charlton Athletic 3, Bradford 1

From Division III to Division I in a couple of seasons is the record Charlton all but made their own by a well-merited victory over Bradford yesterday.

It's long odds against them being pipped. West Ham can just do it, but our money's on Charlton.

Showing smart combination, Charlton called the tune all the time against Bradford. But in view of the strenuous time they had against a relentless attack the Bradford defenders must be given full marks.

Farr effected some fine saves, and the full backs, Lloyd in particular, showed resolution, Danskin did well at centre half, although opposed to a clever centre forward in Prior. The last-named led the Charlton attacks skilfully and scored two fine goals.

REDUCED TO TEN MEN

Bradford's forwards moved quite well when they did get going, Nolan being a thrustful centre. The Charlton defence played splendidly, Joan Oakes, at centre half, again being outstanding, with Welsh a fine attacking half back.

Charlton gained the lead in the first minute, Wilkinson scoring from a centre by Hobbis, Bradford immediately levelled the scores through Nolan following a corner on the left.

Prior regained the advantage for Charlton, and fifteen minutes later scored again.

Bradford fought gamely throughout, particularly in the second half, when they were without Barrett (injured).

Charlton finally claimed Jimmy Seed as their own when they named the north stand – The Valley away end – after him in 1981, 25 years after he was sacked. In the grand North-East football tradition, Seed had been plucked from a life down the Durham pits to play for Sunderland. The First World War ended that fairytale. Four years later, with lungs corrupted by mustard gas, Seed returned to Sunderland, only to be written off as unfit for service on the football field.

Consigned to the game's slagheap in the mining backwater of Mid Rhondda, Seed got his wind back and was signed by Tottenham for £1,000. He won the FA Cup with Spurs in 1921 and played five times for England. After six years, 229 appearances and 64 goals, his reward was a £1 a week pay cut. Aged 32, Seed left for Sheffield Wednesday and was made captain with the Owls seven points adrift at the bottom of Division One and with 10 games left. They survived, and won successive League Championships with Seed.

Seed blazed a trail for today's Redknapps and Savages as a star newspaper columnist in the 1930s. While masterminding the rise of the Addicks, he revealed some of the secrets of his success and his footballing philosophy through his weekly soapbox in the *Mirror* sports pages.

In 1931, Seed became manager of Clapton Orient on the say-so of Arsenal legend Herbert Chapman. In May 1933 he crossed the river to take over at Charlton in the Third Division (South).

Seed told the *Daily Mirror*: "It is too early to predict plans for my new club, and also over-bold to say that Division II will be regained at the first attempt. I have yet to make acquaintance with my playing staff and shall do everything within my scope to make Charlton Athletic a power in Third Division football."

Within three years, Charlton were up there with the elite, the first club to rise from the bottom to the top of the League pyramid in successive seasons, finishing runners-up to the Champions on their Division One debut. And it was all achieved with the same core of players. Charlton were the leading London club in two of their first three seasons in the top flight. There had been fanciful talk of a 200,000-capacity stadium. Seed even tried to buy young Stanley Matthews from Stoke for £13,000.

A Rising Force and Record Crowds

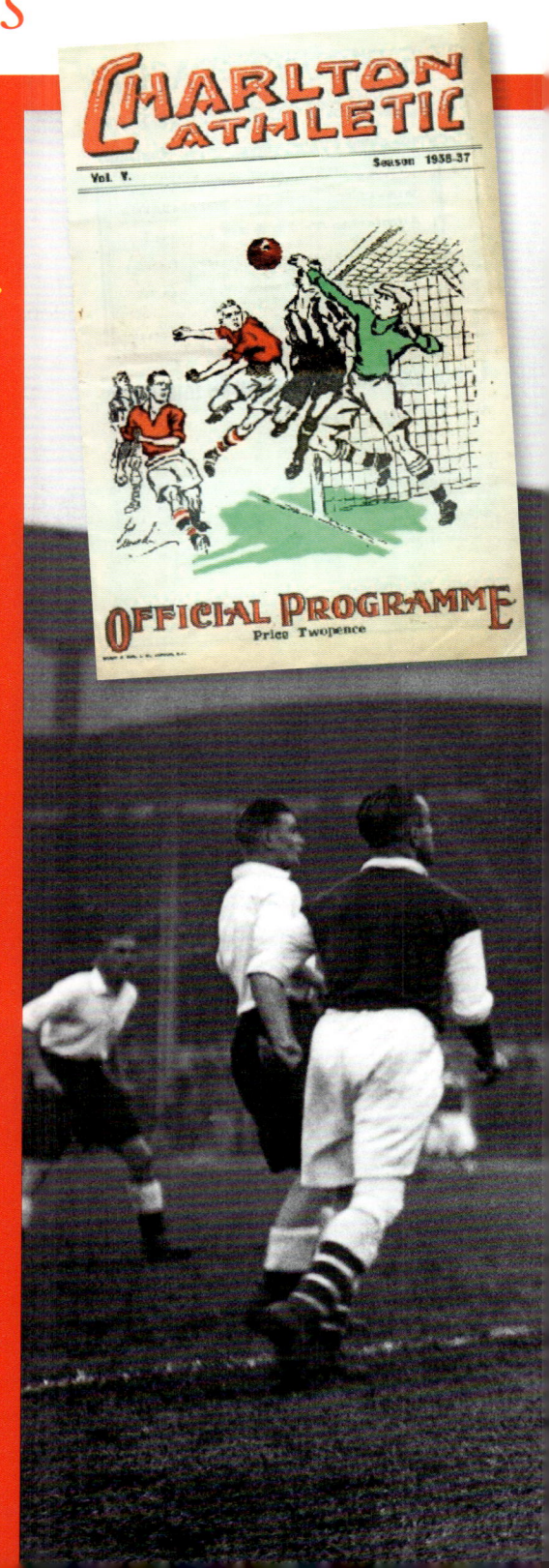

17th May 1933 Jimmy Seed, 38, appointed secretary-manager at relegated Charlton. **30th March 1934** New roofed north stand, the Covered End of Valley legend, is completed for the home match with Reading. **1st December 1934** Sam Bartram's League debut in a 2-0 defeat at Watford. **22nd April 1935** Charlton beat Aldershot 4-0 and guarantee the Division Three (South) title as the Addicks finish eight points clear and Ralph Allen, a £650 buy from Brentford, scores 32 goals in 28 appearances. **2nd May 1936** A 1-1 draw at home to Port Vale seals back-to-back promotions. Charlton finish Division Two runners-up to Manchester United. **5th September 1936** Charlton draw 1-1 with Liverpool in the first top-flight game at The Valley. The match programme (above right) envisages a 40–50,000 crowd. In fact the attendance is 31,301. **17th October 1936** The visit of Arsenal attracts Charlton's record League attendance of 68,160. The *Mirror's* man says: "I wonder the spectators perched like crows on the roofs of the stands did not fall off in their excitement." The Gunners win 2-0. **May 1937** The Addicks finish runners-up in their debut First Division season, three points behind Manchester City. **12th February 1938** Record Valley crowd of 75,031 in attendance for the 1-1 FA Cup fifth-round tie with Aston Villa. **11th February 1939** Charlton 7-1 Manchester United – a record win at the time, with George Tadman scoring four.

LEFT: In his white coat, Jimmy Trotter looks more suited to leading the greyhounds out at Walthamstow. He became Charlton trainer in 1934, having played with Jimmy Seed at Sheffield Wednesday where he topped the First Division goalscoring charts in 1926–27.

RIGHT: On 30th September 1938 Neville Chamberlain declares "peace for our time" at Heston Aerodrome after appeasing Hitler in Munich. The following day, 1st October, the British Prime Minister sees Charlton's 4-4 draw with Birmingham City at The Valley, where the local rector offers a thanksgiving prayer and a crowd of 20,000 sing along to 'Land of Hope and Glory'.

Charlton play a midweek afternoon London Challenge Cup tie in front of a few hundred at Highbury on 7th October 1935, a year before the two sides met for the first time in front of The Valley's biggest League crowd.

Legends of the Rise

The following pages are dedicated to the players who launched Charlton on the path to glory in the prewar years. Less than two decades on from the club's nomadic non-League days, the Addicks were a top-four fixture in Division One.

Workers would pour out of the factories beside the Thames after a 47-hour week – 30,000 employees at Woolwich Arsenal alone – and pay their tanner or a bob to get into The Valley. Their Saturday afternoon heroes arrived by trolleybus, tram or even push-bike, just like the fans – although Don Welsh had a car and charged the other players a penny or two for a lift up and down Charlton Church Lane!

A young Valley regular of the time tells of his feet hardly touching the ground till reaching Charlton station in the mass exodus after the final whistle. A penny raffle ticket could win you the match ball, which one lucky punter described as like carrying a lead weight home after a particularly wet afternoon at The Valley.

Home and away supporters stood together and the police presence comprised a bobby sat on a stool by each corner flag.

Bartram, Welsh, Turner, Tadman – some of the names that evoke sepia-toned memories, players deprived of the best years of their careers by Adolf Hitler, but who did Charlton proud.

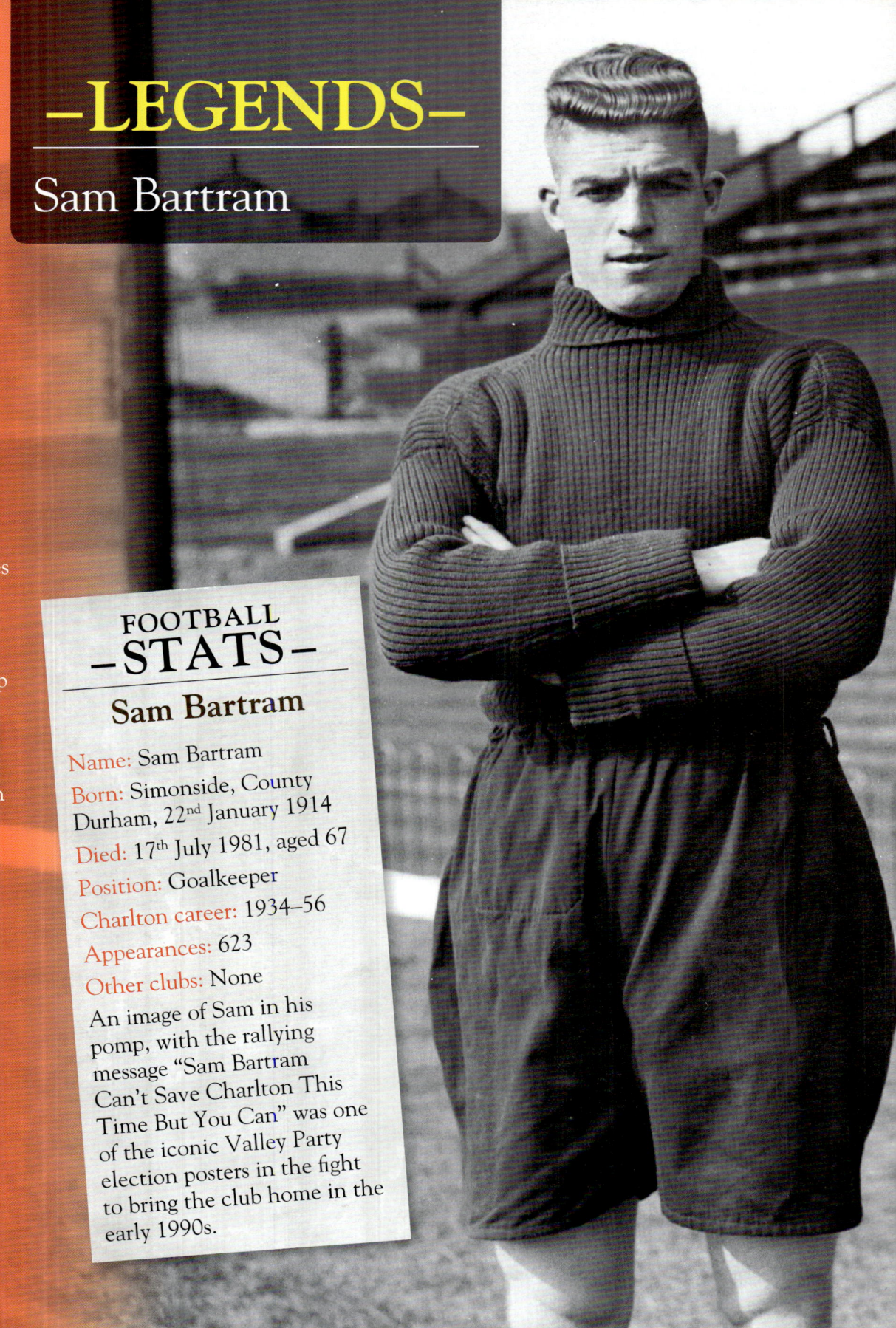

–LEGENDS–

Sam Bartram

FOOTBALL –STATS–

Sam Bartram

Name: Sam Bartram
Born: Simonside, County Durham, 22nd January 1914
Died: 17th July 1981, aged 67
Position: Goalkeeper
Charlton career: 1934–56
Appearances: 623
Other clubs: None

An image of Sam in his pomp, with the rallying message "Sam Bartram Can't Save Charlton This Time But You Can" was one of the iconic Valley Party election posters in the fight to bring the club home in the early 1990s.

–LEGENDS–

Bert Turner

FOOTBALL –STATS–

Bert Turner

Name: Bert Turner
Born: Brithdir, Wales, 19th June 1909
Died: Birchington, Kent, 8th June 1981, aged 71
Position: Full-back
Charlton career: 1933–46
Appearances: 196
Goals: 4
Other clubs: None

Bert won eight Wales caps and when his Charlton career ended he managed Swedish club Malmö to two League titles and two domestic cups.

CHURCHMAN'S CIGARETTES

H. TURNER (CHARLTON ATHLETIC)

–LEGENDS–

John Oakes

FOOTBALL –STATS–

John Oakes

Name: John Oakes

Born: Winsford, Cheshire, 13th September 1905

Died: March 1992, aged 86

Position: Centre-half

Charlton career: 1936–46

Appearances: 145

Goals: 3

Other clubs: Nottingham Forest, Southend, Aldershot, Plymouth Argyle

As tough as old 1930s boots, Oakes cost £650 from Aldershot, but turned out to be such an asset that Charlton ended up giving the Hampshire club an extra £499!

Don Welsh

> " Don played in all the
> key positions . . .
> Charlton never had a
> better or stronger
> utility player. Looking
> back on the years he
> would have been worth
> £30,000 to the club. "
>
> Jimmy Seed

FOOTBALL –STATS–

Don Welsh

Name: Don Welsh

Born: Manchester, 25th February 1911

Died: Stevenage, 2nd February 1990, aged 78

Position: Forward; half-back

Charlton career: 1935–47

Appearances: 216

Goals: 50

Other clubs: Torquay United

Signed for a club record £3,250, he captained Charlton to four Wembley finals, including wartime ones in 1943 and 1944, and played three times for England.

31

–LEGENDS–
Monty Wilkinson

–LEGENDS–
George Tadman

FOOTBALL –STATS–
Monty Wilkinson

Name: Monty Wilkinson

Born: Esh Winning, County Durham, 18th July 1908

Died: Newcastle, 19th September 1979, aged 71

Position: Forward

Charlton career: 1933–39

Appearances: 235

Goals: 50

Other clubs: Newcastle United, Everton, Blackpool

Wilkinson spent two seasons as Hughie Gallacher's understudy at Newcastle before two more seasons at Everton where opportunities were limited by another goalscoring phenomenon – none other than 60-goals-in-a-season Dixie Dean. He made a telling contribution to Charlton's historic rise, mainly from the right-wing.

FOOTBALL –STATS–
George Tadman

Name: George Tadman

Born: Rainham, Kent, 5th November 1914

Died: Bristol, 28th September 1994, aged 79

Position: Winger; centre-forward

Charlton career: 1936–39

Appearances: 93

Goals: 50

Other clubs: Gillingham

No player perhaps epitomizes how the Second World War blighted so many Charlton careers than Tadman. In the last peacetime season he plundered 24 goals in 31 games, including a spell of eight in four matches. He began 1939–40 with two in three outings before the season was shut down. Still only 24, Tadman never played another Football League game.

Cup results of February 1938 show the record attendance for a match at The Valley. Although the final figure was adjusted down by 1,000, the actual receipts shed a disturbing light on the club's finances. Arsenal had several thousand fewer fans at their tie against Preston, yet their takings were nearly double those of Charlton. Liverpool and Sunderland, with almost 20,000 fewer through the gates, also brought in more money.

The FA Cup fifth-round tie against Aston Villa went to two replays and was watched by 201,343 people in total. Villa came back from two down in the first replay at Villa Park, leaving Jimmy Seed to complain that the referee, Mr Twist, "rather favoured the home side, especially in the law of fouls".

George Tadman gave Charlton the lead in the second replay, in front of a crowd of 64,782 at neutral Highbury on a Monday afternoon in February. Two minutes later, Harold Hobbis suffered a broken right leg. The 10 men of Charlton were pegged back early in the second half and went 2-1 down in the 84th minute, before being reduced to nine when Tadman was injured. Two more goals rubbed salt into Charlton wounds as Villa went through 4-1.

F.A. CUP—FIFTH ROUND

Arsenal	0	Preston N.E.	1	Liverpool	0	Huddersfield	1
		Dougal				Barclay	
Attendance 72,121		Receipts £7,214		Attendance 57,582		Receipts £4,107	
Brentford	2	Man. Utd.	0	Luton	1	Man. City	3
Holliday, Reid				Payne		Heale, Doherty,	
Attendance 27,147		Receipts £2,021				Nelson o.g.	
				Attendance 21,899		Receipts £2,873	
Charlton	1	Aston Villa	1	Sunderland	1	Bradford	0
Robinson		Shell		Duns			
Attendance 76,031		Receipts £5,920		Attendance 69,226		Receipts £5,932	
Chesterfield	2	Tottenham	2	York City	1	Middlesbro'	0
Clifton, Sliman		Gibbons, Miller		Spooner			
Attendance 30,561		Receipts £2,037		Attendance 23,860		Receipts £3,192	

Tadman training at The Valley in September 1938. When Don Welsh named the best team over the years he spent at Charlton between 1935 and 1947, he had no hesitation in picking Tadman – and himself! His full line-up was: Sam Bartram, Bert Turner, Jimmy Oakes (captain), Frank Harris, John Oakes, Don Welsh, Monty Wilkinson, Sailor Brown, George Tadman, Les Boulter, Harold Hobbis or Chris Duffy.

Jimmy Oakes

Les Boulter

FOOTBALL –STATS–

Jimmy Oakes

Name: Jimmy Oakes

Born: Hanley, Staffordshire, 5th November 1902

Died: Stoke-on-Trent, 7th November 1992, aged 90

Position: Left-back

Charlton career: 1933–39

Appearances: 234

Goals: 0

Other clubs: Port Vale

Oakes was a two-club man who ended up playing for both of them in the same match. After starting for Vale in a fixture against Charlton that was eventually abandoned, he was transferred to The Valley before the rearranged game took place!

FOOTBALL –STATS–

Les Boulter

Name: Les Boulter

Born: Ebbw Vale, 31st August 1913

Died: Pwllheli, 14th November 1975, aged 62

Position: Forward

Charlton career: 1933–39

Appearances: 175

Goals: 29

Other clubs: Brentford, Yeovil

Boulter, who cost nothing, was sold to Brentford in 1939 for £5,950.

George Green, on the left, arrived at Charlton in 1934, but before he had kicked a ball for the first team he was wooed away to Espanyol, who offered a £100 signing-on fee and double the wages. His Spanish adventure was cut short by the Civil War and he came back to play 63 times for Charlton and win four caps as a half-back for Wales. Charlie Drinkwater, on the right, made just three starts as a winger for Charlton.

FOOTBALL –STATS–

George Robinson

Name: George Robinson

Born: Marlpool, Derbyshire, 11th January 1908

Died: Blackheath, 15th January 1963, aged 55

Position: Inside-right

Charlton career: 1931–47

Appearances: 254

Goals: 45

Other clubs: Sunderland

Robinson was packed off to Birmingham & District League side Burton Town after a less-than-distinguished start at The Valley, but Seed rescued the inside-forward and Robinson played all but one game as Charlton rose through the divisions. He missed a single match in the debut Division One season.

> "Sailor used to go missing before the players went out for each game. He would be in the toilet having a quiet five minutes with a Woodbine. He was such a good player, the manager took no notice.
>
> Sam Bartram"

'Sailor' Brown

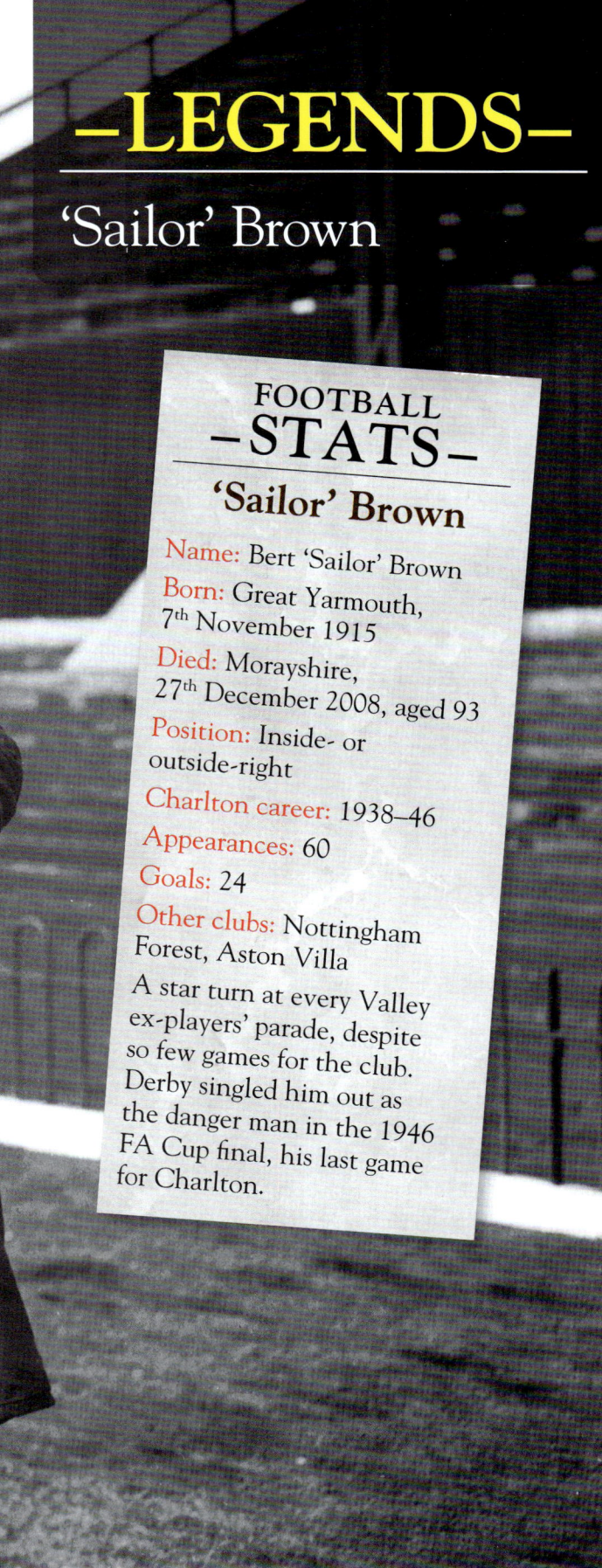

FOOTBALL –STATS–

'Sailor' Brown

Name: Bert 'Sailor' Brown

Born: Great Yarmouth, 7th November 1915

Died: Morayshire, 27th December 2008, aged 93

Position: Inside- or outside-right

Charlton career: 1938–46

Appearances: 60

Goals: 24

Other clubs: Nottingham Forest, Aston Villa

A star turn at every Valley ex-players' parade, despite so few games for the club. Derby singled him out as the danger man in the 1946 FA Cup final, his last game for Charlton.

Tale of the Tables

DIVISION III (S.)

Bournemouth	0	Queen's P.R.	2	
Bristol C.	4	Cardiff	0	
Clapton Orient	3	Southend	0	
Coventry	1	Luton	0	
Exeter	8	Aldershot	1	
Gillingham	1	Bristol R.	1	
Millwall	3	Brighton	1	
Newport	1	Swindon	2	
Northampton	3	Crystal Palace	2	
Reading	2	Charlton	2	
Watford	3			

	P.	W.	D.	L.	F.	A.	Pts.
Charlton Athletic	42	27	7	8	103	52	61
Reading	42	21	11	10	89	65	53
Coventry City	42	21	9	12	86	50	51
Luton Town	42	19	12	11	92	60	50
Crystal Palace	42	19	10	13	86	64	48
Watford	42	19	9	14	76	49	47
Northampton Town	42	19	8	15	65	67	46
Bristol Rovers	42	17	10	15	73	77	44
Brighton and H. A.	42	18	6	18	69	62	43
Torquay United	42	18	6	18	81	75	42
Exeter City	42	16	9	17	70	75	41
Millwall	42	17	7	18	57	62	41
Queen's Park R.	42	16	9	17	63	72	41
Clapton Orient	42	15	10	17	65	65	40
Bristol City	42	15	9	18	52	68	39
Swindon Town	42	13	12	17	67	78	38
Bournemouth	42	15	7	20	54	71	37
Aldershot	42	13	10	19	50	75	36
Cardiff City	42	13	9	20	62	82	35
Gillingham	42	11	13	18	55	75	35
Southend United	42	11	9	22	65	78	31
Newport County	42	10	5	27	54	112	25

DIVISION II

Barnsley	0	Tottenham	0	
Bradford City	2	Leicester	0	
Travis, Murphy				
Burnley	0	Fulham	2	
		Perry, Arnold		
Charlton	1	Port Vale	1	
Hobbis		Caldwell		
Hull	1	Manchester Utd.	1	
Acquroff		Bamford		
Norwich	2	Doncaster	1	
Vinall, Warnes		Barlow		
Plymouth	1	Newcastle	0	
Prescott				
Sheffield Utd.	4	West Ham	2	
Conway, Barclay 2, Dodds		Foreman, Marshall		
Swansea	1	Bradford	2	
Bram		Robertson, Lewis		

		HOME			AWAY			GOALS		
	P.	W.	D.	L.	W.	D.	L.	F.	A.	Pts.
Man. Utd.	42	22	12	8	16	3	2	6	9	85 43	56
Charlton	42	22	11	9	15	6	0	7	5	9 85 58	55
Shef. Utd.	42	20	12	10	15	4	3	5	8	79 50	52
West Ham	42	22	8	12	13	5	3	9	9	90 68	52
Spars	42	18	13	11	12	5	2	5	5	11 79 55	49
Leicester	42	19	10	13	14	5	2	5	5	11 79 57	48
Plymouth	42	20	11	11	15	2	4	5	6	10 71 57	48
Newcastle	42	20	6	16	13	5	3	7	1	13 88 79	46
Fulham	42	15	14	13	11	6	4	4	8	9 76 52	44
Blackpool	42	15	16	11	11	3	4	4	13	93 72	43
Norwich	42	17	9	16	14	2	5	3	7	11 72 65	43
Bradford C.	42	15	13	14	12	7	2	5	5	12 67 76	39
Swansea	42	15	9	18	11	5	7	4	6	11 67 76	39
Bury	42	15	12	17	10	6	8	5	6	12 66 84	38
Bradford	42	15	17	10	8	4	5	3	15	50 69	37
Burnley	42	14	11	12	13	6	2	1	3	17 62 84	37
Southampton	42	14	9	19	11	7	3	6	17	47 65	37
Doncaster	42	14	9	19	10	7	4	4	2	15 51 71	37
N. Forest	42	12	11	15	8	6	2	5	3	17 76 35	35
Barnsley	42	12	9	21	9	4	8	3	5	13 54 80	35
Port Vale	42	12	8	22	10	9	5	2	3	17 56 106	32
Hull	42	5	10	27	4	7	10	1	3	17 47 111	20

F.A. CUP FINAL

Preston North End	1	Sunderland	3

DIVISION I

Arsenal	0	Bolton Wanderers	0
Birmingham	2	Manchester City	2
Charlton Athletic	2	Brentford	1
Grimsby Town	1	Stoke City	3
Huddersfield	1	Sheffield Wednesday	0
Leeds United	1	Portsmouth	1
Liverpool	1	Chelsea	1
West Bromwich A.	3	Middlesbrough	1
Wolverhampton	3	Derby County	1

		Home.			Away.			Goals.		
	P.	W.	D.	L.	W.	D.	L.	F.	A.	Pts.
Manchester C.	42	15	5	1	7	8	6	107	61	57
Charlton	42	15	5	1	6	7	8	58	49	54
Arsenal	42	10	10	1	8	7	6	80	49	52
Derby	42	12	3	5	8	4	9	96	90	49
Wolves	42	16	3	2	5	3	13	84	67	47
Brentford	42	13	2	4	5	12	82	78	46
Middlesbro'	42	14	6	1	5	2	14	74	71	46
Sunderland	42	17	2	2	4	15	89	87	44
Portsmouth	42	13	3	5	7	10	62	66	44
Stoke	42	12	6	3	3	6	12	72	57	42
Birmingham	42	13	5	3	4	13	86	81	41
Grimsby	42	9	7	5	4	8	9	64	60	41
Chelsea	42	11	6	3	5	7	11	52	55	41
Preston	42	10	6	5	7	10	56	67	41
Huddersfield	42	13	5	4	0	10	11	62	64	39
West Brom. A.	42	13	5	3	3	15	77	98	38
Everton	42	12	5	2	2	17	81	78	37
Liverpool	42	9	8	4	5	15	62	84	35
Leeds	42	14	3	4	1	19	60	80	34
Bolton	42	6	6	9	4	8	9	43	66	34
Manchester U.	42	8	9	4	2	3	16	55	78	32
Sheffield Wed.	42	8	5	8	1	7	13	53	69	30

The tables tell the remarkable Charlton story. Division Three (South) Champions in 1934–35, then second in Division Two and runners-up in the top flight a year later. As the curtain came down on the 1935–36 campaign, the *Mirror* commented: "Afterthoughts on the football season lead one inevitably to the question of finance. Charlton have won promotion for the second time. The same team that took them into the second division last year has now carried them into the first in record quick time. They have spent less than £4,000 on players in their two-seasons' climb. Aston Villa are going down into the second division for the first time in their career after spending £40,000 and more."

The vast sweep of the East Terrace, rising to the clouds in 132 steps, still had rattle-twirling room to spare on 27th December 1937, when 51,125 saw Charlton beat Chelsea 3-1. The concreting-over of those rugged sandy heights cemented The Valley's pre-eminence as the biggest Football League ground in the land. These were the days before all-ticket matches, when the gates were simply locked if the ground was full. Charlton never had to lock the gates.

Tragedies Cast a Shadow

The 1934–35 season was memorable for the start of Charlton's rise. A midweek trip to Torquay on 6th September 1934, resulted in a narrow 2-1 win that put the Addicks top of Division Three (South). The star of the show was their Scottish goalie Alex 'Sanny' Wright, who had made the jersey his own since 1932.

The players went for a dip in the sea the next morning before catching the train back to London. Wright, 29, broke his neck diving from a wooden bathing raft off Torre Abbey Sands, unaware of how shallow the sea was at low tide.

His mother and fiancée arrived from Glasgow the next morning, just 10 minutes before he died. Wright's sister spoke of their anguish: "I am so sorry for Miss Margaret Calderwood," she said. "They have been sweethearts for six years and became engaged three years ago. They hoped to be married at the close of the football season. She is very like him in nature and very rarely mixed in other company. Alec seemed to be her sole interest in life. I don't know what she will do now.

"Miss Calderwood rushed down to Torquay with my father and mother when we heard of the accident and she was with Alec when he died. Mother, too, is heartbroken . . . she was afraid to let him go back at the beginning of the season. She had a feeling something would happen to him."

The tragedy brought 15,000 people out on to the streets of Wright's home town of Kilmarnock to line the three-mile route of his cortège. Jimmy Seed and two team-mates attended the funeral. Albert Gliksten, the Charlton chairman, paid tribute to the young man, saying: "He was a great fellow, liked by everyone, and he had a brilliant football career in front of him." Floral tributes included wreaths in the shape of goalposts with nets fashioned from flowers of many colours.

Alex Wright.

FOOTBALLER'S FATAL DIVE

Bathing Mishap Costs Alex Wright His Life

Alex Wright, Charlton Athletic's Scottish goalkeeper, who received severe spinal injuries in diving from a raft into shallow water at Torre Abbey sands, died yesterday in Torbay Hospital, Torquay.

His mother and sister, travelling all night from Glasgow, reached the hospital ten minutes before he died.

Wright was bathing with other members of the Charlton team. His head hit the bottom with terrific force and his spine was fractured near the neck.

The previous night he had played for his team against Torquay United.

The Courage of George Green

A heart-rending scene with the coffin of Charlton wing-half George Green's 18-month-old son Brian, borne upon the shoulders of his team-mates Don Welsh, Jack Shreeve and John Oakes.

Green discovered his little boy's lifeless body in a neighbour's garden pond in October 1938. Four hours later he heard he had been called up to play for Wales. Two days after the funeral, where his wife collapsed sobbing her little lad's name, Green won his first cap as the Welsh side beat England 4-2.

Green explained his decision to get on with his footballing life so soon after the tragedy: "It is my living simply, and it will help me to try to forget what I have lost," he said. "Brian was worth a million pounds to me. He was the greatest little kid that ever lived. I used to take him to the Valley when reserve matches were being played and he would cheer and clap with the rest of the crowd."

Carried by members of Charlton Athletic Football Club, and with the parents' wreaths resting on top, the coffin of eighteen-month-old Brian George Green leaving 31, Rochester-way.

Three of the bearers are: Donald Welsh (head of coffin), Jack Shreeve (centre of picture) and John Oakes (open coat).

FOOTBALL CAP ON SADDEST DAY OF HIS LIFE

THE reward that every footballer dreams of—his international cap—came yesterday to George Henry Green, twenty-three, who plays for Charlton Athletic Club, but when it came it found Green a broken man.

Four hours before he learned that he had been picked to play for Wales next Saturday Green had lifted the body of his only son Brian, aged eighteen months, from an ornamental fish pond in the garden adjacent to his home in Rochester-way, Blackheath.

A fence divides the garden from the house, and it had been arranged for Mr. Green to pull it down yesterday morning and erect another in its place.

He had been playing happily with Brian in his garden. Then he spoke to the neighbour, Mr. Grant, and started to pull down the fence.

Brian wandered into the neighbour's kitchen, where Mrs. Grant gave him a biscuit. Brian disappeared, and Mrs. Grant thought he had gone back home.

It was not until Mrs. Constance Green called to her husband to send Brian in that the baby's disappearance was noticed.

"The greatest little kid that ever lived . . ." Brian Green, eighteen months, whose father picked him from an ornamental fish pond—dead.

Fixture pile-ups, playing two games a week, Premier League managers with their 25-man squads complaining about burnout? Go back to 10th April 1939, and Charlton are playing their third match in four days over Easter. And they won them all. After 2-0 and 1-0 victories over Chelsea and Aston Villa at The Valley, the Addicks went to Stamford Bridge and made it three on the bounce. Ten of the 11 who beat Chelsea 3-1 played all three games. Here Sam Bartram safely clutches the ball watched by Jimmy and John Oakes with Pensioners (as Chelsea were once proud to be called) inside-forward Jimmy Argue lurking.

A golf day at Sundridge Park before Charlton's third-round FA Cup tie against Third Division Cardiff. Monty Wilkinson is playing out of a bunker, watched by (left to right) Harold Hobbis, Sam Bartram and Bert Turner. Below, Don Welsh hangs on to Bert Tann as he tries to retrieve his ball from the drink while John Cakes looks on. Three days later, on 7th January 1939, the Addicks were dumped out of the competition 1-0 at Ninian Park in the shock of the round.

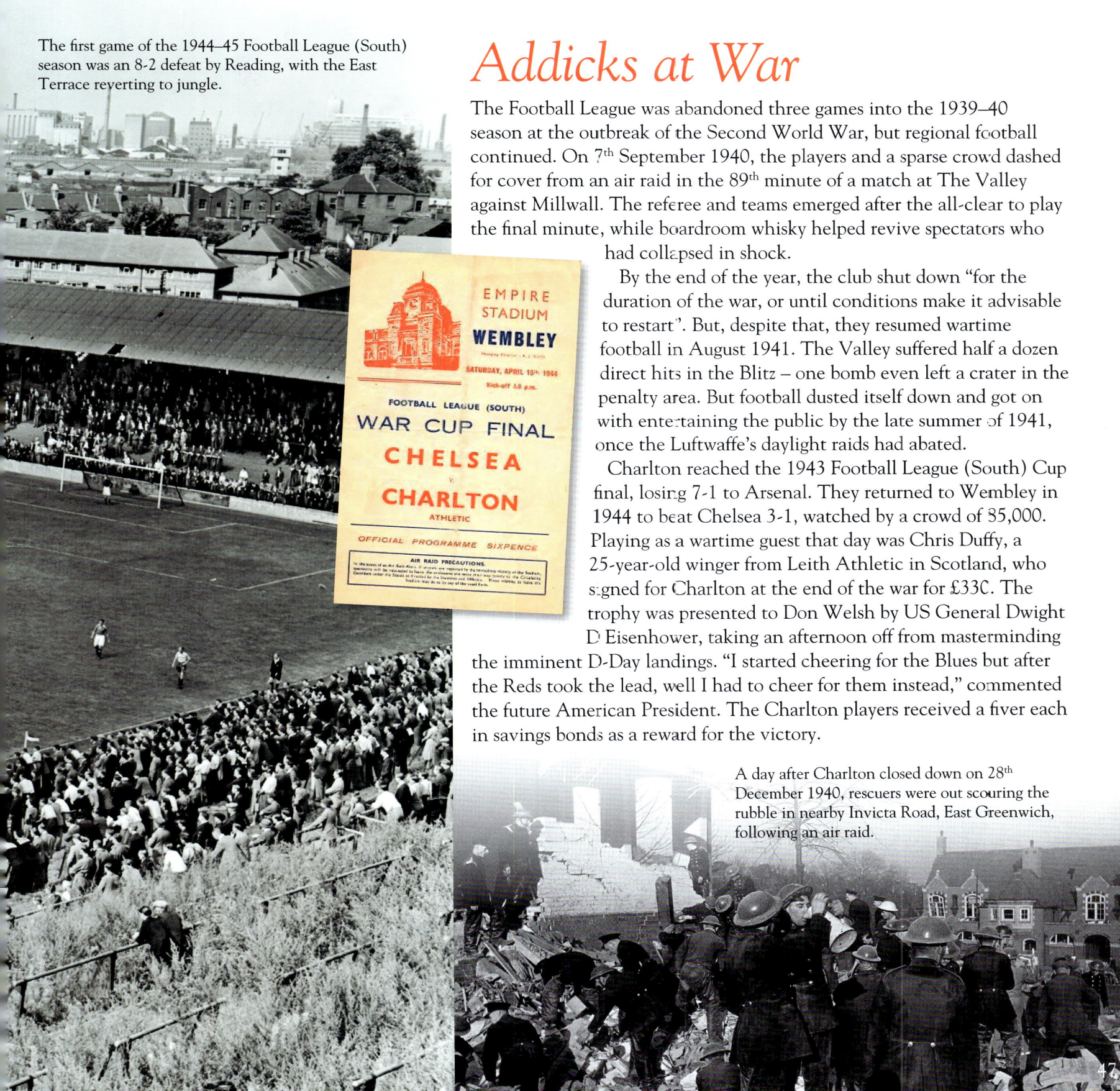

The first game of the 1944–45 Football League (South) season was an 8-2 defeat by Reading, with the East Terrace reverting to jungle.

EMPIRE STADIUM WEMBLEY

Managing Director · A.J. Elvin

SATURDAY, APRIL 15th 1944
Kick-off 3.0 p.m.

FOOTBALL LEAGUE (SOUTH)

WAR CUP FINAL

CHELSEA
v.
CHARLTON
ATHLETIC

OFFICIAL PROGRAMME SIXPENCE

AIR RAID PRECAUTIONS.

Addicks at War

The Football League was abandoned three games into the 1939–40 season at the outbreak of the Second World War, but regional football continued. On 7th September 1940, the players and a sparse crowd dashed for cover from an air raid in the 89th minute of a match at The Valley against Millwall. The referee and teams emerged after the all-clear to play the final minute, while boardroom whisky helped revive spectators who had collapsed in shock.

By the end of the year, the club shut down "for the duration of the war, or until conditions make it advisable to restart". But, despite that, they resumed wartime football in August 1941. The Valley suffered half a dozen direct hits in the Blitz – one bomb even left a crater in the penalty area. But football dusted itself down and got on with entertaining the public by the late summer of 1941, once the Luftwaffe's daylight raids had abated.

Charlton reached the 1943 Football League (South) Cup final, losing 7-1 to Arsenal. They returned to Wembley in 1944 to beat Chelsea 3-1, watched by a crowd of 85,000. Playing as a wartime guest that day was Chris Duffy, a 25-year-old winger from Leith Athletic in Scotland, who signed for Charlton at the end of the war for £330. The trophy was presented to Don Welsh by US General Dwight D Eisenhower, taking an afternoon off from masterminding the imminent D-Day landings. "I started cheering for the Blues but after the Reds took the lead, well I had to cheer for them instead," commented the future American President. The Charlton players received a fiver each in savings bonds as a reward for the victory.

A day after Charlton closed down on 28th December 1940, rescuers were out scouring the rubble in nearby Invicta Road, East Greenwich, following an air raid.

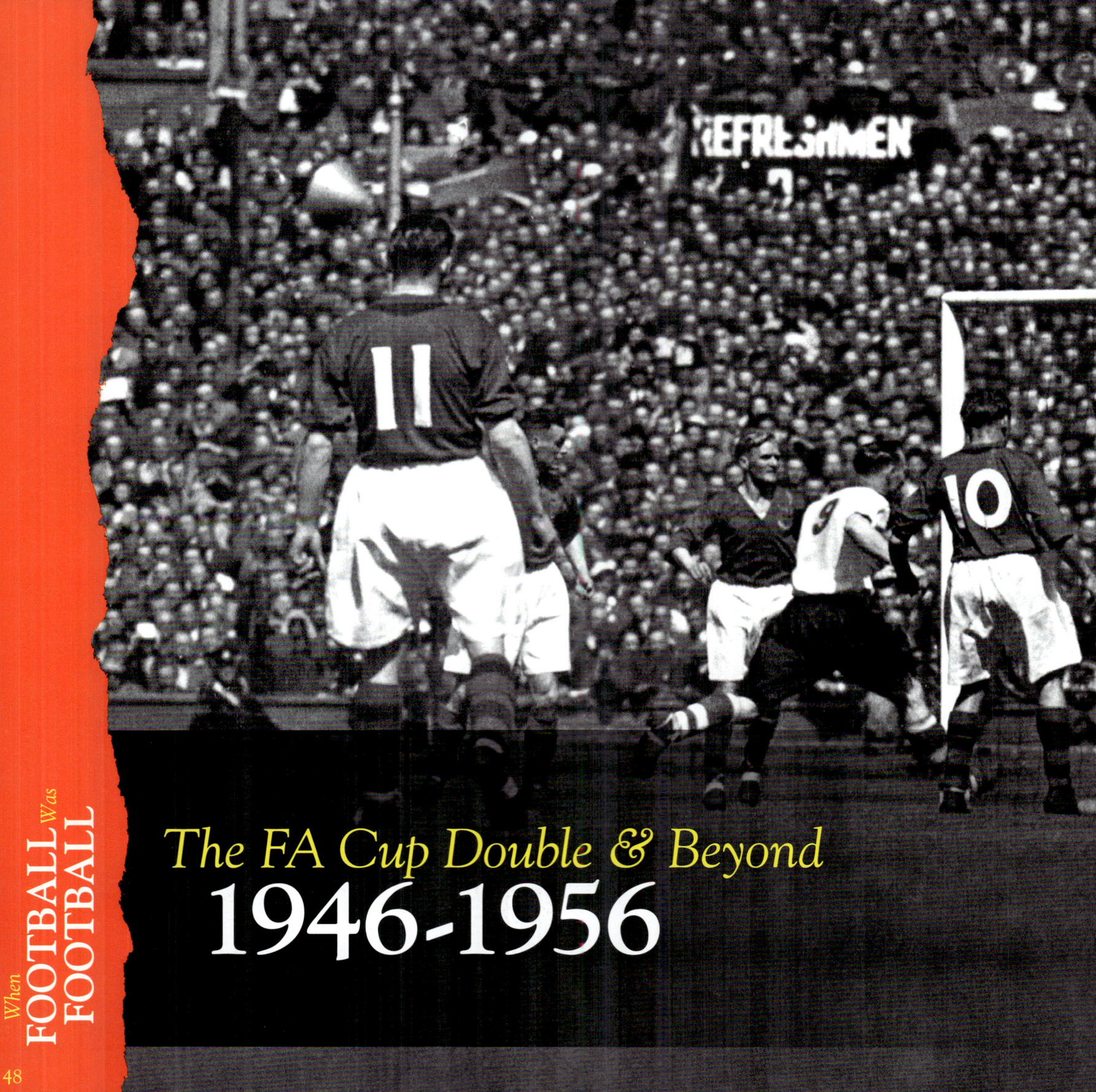

When **FOOTBALL** *Was* **FOOTBALL**

The FA Cup Double & Beyond
1946-1956

“*We were probably the only team to arrive for a Cup final with shirts and shorts but no socks.*”

Charlton right-back Peter Crcker

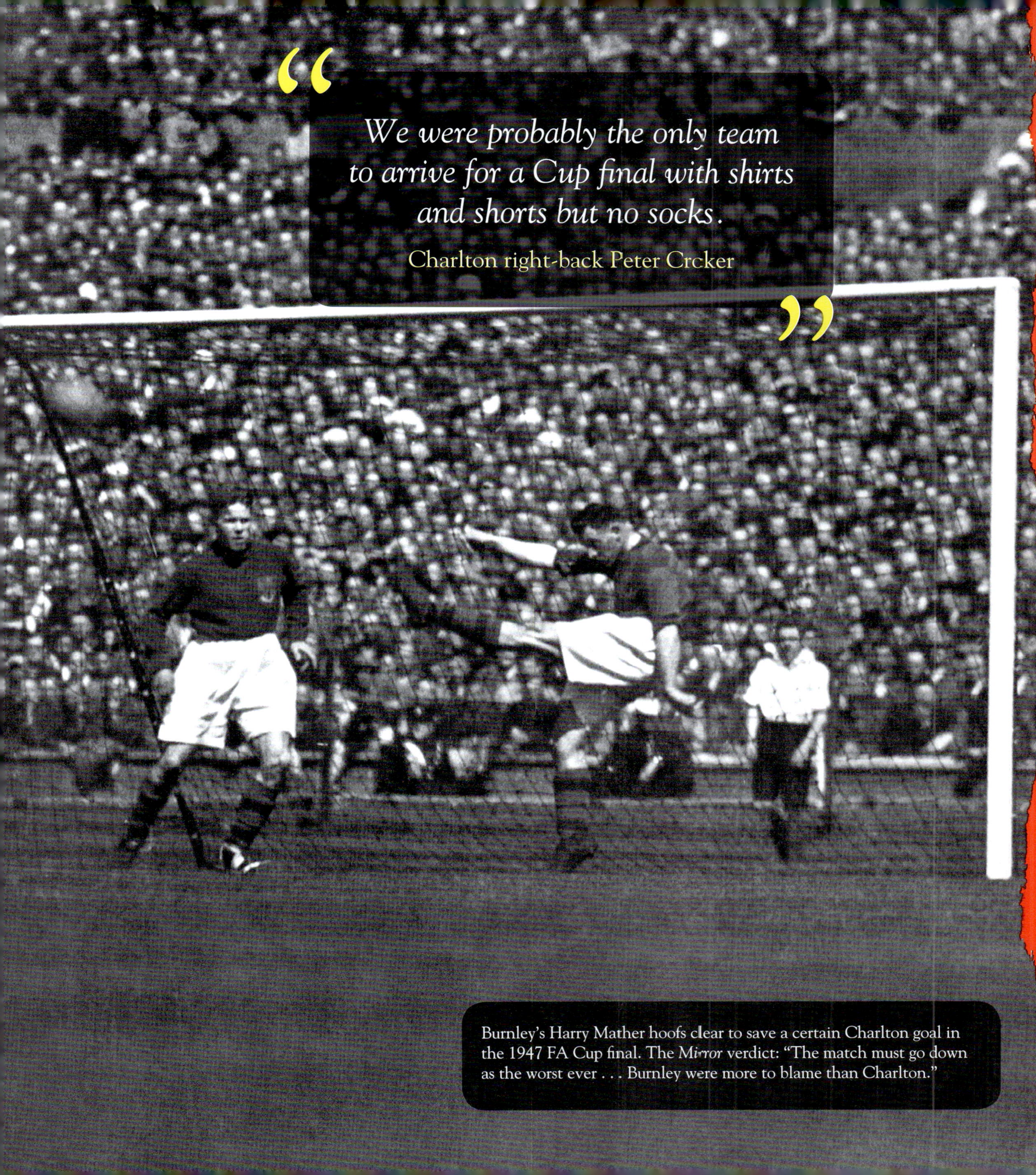

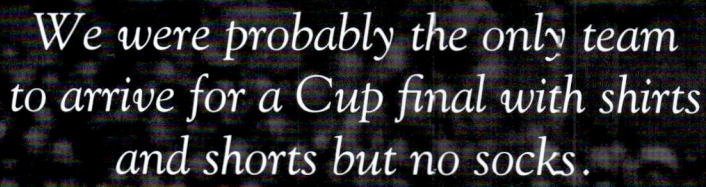

Burnley’s Harry Mather hoofs clear to save a certain Charlton goal in the 1947 FA Cup final. The *Mirror* verdict: “The match must go down as the worst ever . . . Burnley were more to blame than Charlton.”

Wembley's a Second Home

After their Football League War Cup heroics, Charlton played in the first two peacetime FA Cup finals, creating history and some oddly unique folklore along the Wembley way. Fans too young to have been there – which means everyone but a vanishing few – know the stories that have become pub sports quiz staples:

- Charlton are the only club to reach an FA Cup final after losing in the third round.
- Bert Turner of Charlton is the first player to score for both sides in a final.
- The ball bursts in both finals.
- The 1946 finalists each receive two medals.

The 1946 FA Cup competition was played over two legs and Charlton beat Fulham 4-3 on aggregate, winning 3-1 at The Valley before going down 2-1 at Craven Cottage. They reached Wembley with a 2-0 semi-final victory over Bolton in front of a crowd of 70,819 at Villa Park. In the nine days before facing Derby County, Charlton played six Football League (South) games.

The final remained goalless until Turner skewed an attempted clearance past Bartram in the 85th minute. It took only a minute for the Charlton man to redeem himself from a free-kick on the edge of the Derby area. As well as being the first to score at both ends, Turner was also the oldest player to score in an FA Cup final, at 36 years and 312 days. It finished 1-1 after 90 minutes but Derby romped away to win 4-1 in extra-time, two of the goals coming from Jack Stamp, whose fierce shot close to the end of normal time left Bartram clutching a deflated lump of leather.

Charlton's Arthur Turner, who never kicked a ball in the Football League for the club, was the first amateur to play in an FA Cup final for 20 years. Three years earlier, he was the only survivor from the six-man crew of an RAF bomber shot down off the coast of Spain.

For the presentation, the players had to make do with bronze medals, but received gold ones later when rationing of the precious metal was eased.

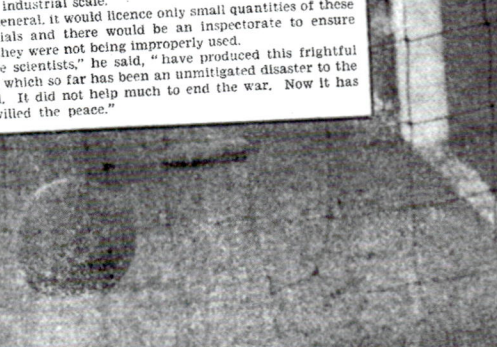

Sunday Pictoria[l]

AMERICA IS SHARE ATO SECRET

There is agony writte[n] the Charlton full back, net off the boot of his first goal that led to t[he] even more h[...]

A MERICA IS READY TO HAND OVER TO THE UNITED NATIONS CONTROL OF THE SECRET OF ATOMIC BOMBS AND ATOMIC POWER.

This dramatic end to months of doubt and fear which had threatened to disrupt the peace of the world came in a disclosure last night by Professor P. M. S. Blackett, member of the British atomic research team and head of the physics department of Manchester University, in a speech at Manchester yesterday.

Scientists, production technicians and engineers from all the chief countries of the world —this presumably includes Russia—will form an international administration body to develop atom power.

Professor Blackett said that the report of the American State Department—the United States Foreign Office—on the international control of atomic energy which will be published in Britain in the next few days will recommend the formation of such an international Committee, and that it will be known as the Atomic Development Research Administration.

Dangerous Jobs

The body would also be responsible for all dangerous research operations such as the mining of uranium—the ore from which the essential of the atom bomb is derived —and the erection of uranium piles, the system of converting atomic energy to peace-time uses.

Professor Blackett said the organisation would sell, or hand over, to national authorities or private enterprise the materials necessary for the exploitation of atomic energy on an industrial scale.

In general, it would licence only small quantities of these materials and there would be an inspectorate to ensure that they were not being improperly used.

"We scientists," he said, "have produced this frightful thing which so far has been an unmitigated disaster to the world. It did not help much to end the war. Now it has bedevilled the peace."

April 28, 1946.
No. 1,624
TWOPENCE

Boycott the Salad Robbers
PAGE 11

EADY TO

Oh, the Agony of It All!

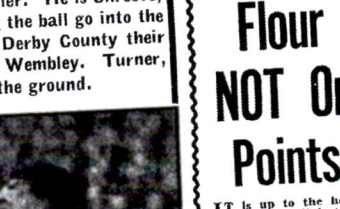

this footballer. He is Shreeve, watching the ball go into the —to give Derby County their Cup win at Wembley. Turner, de him on the ground.

Flour NOT On Points

IT is up to the housewives of Britain to see that nobody goes short of bread. So long as they do not panic and think they are being clever by buying more bread than they need there will be no shortage.

And just to show the housewives that they are trusted to play the game the Government last night announced that flour is not to go on points.

Nor is there to be any cut in the supply of breakfast cereals

There will be just as much flour available for home baking of cakes and cooking of puddings as before. There will be no restrictions on its purchase—so long as the housewives do not go crazy and buy more than they normally do and end up by wasting it.

THE Government decision not to put flour on points and to leave breakfast cereals alone was made in an announcement last night that the only points changes for the new period concern —Camembert cheese and Matzos

Supplies of Camembert are coming from France in the next few months The cheeses will cost 7 apiece and will be procurable for six point Average weight of a Camembert is about 1lb.

Change in the point value of Matzos (Jewish ceremonial biscuits) lows the end of the P over season. They now require two points pound.

That—with cheese biscuits—is the end of "flour-on-points" you have been rea during the week.

AND along with i get the scare wheat going bad in The National Assoc of British and Iris lers say it just isn't

But you must k your watch on was! Tom Williams, Minister of Agriculture, said yesterday our crisis would last a year.

All next winter the need to cut bread consumption would be just as great

NO · STAR 1 57

Sunday Pictorial
No. 1,676
Twopence

Page Six: New facts about
VICE IN LONDON

CUP FEVER

This is the picture that tells the whole Cup Final story—Charlton's captain, Don Welsh, is chaired and cheered as he carries off the prize. Twice running Charlton played extra time in the Final, yesterday beating Burnley 1—0.
★

Full Report: Back Page

Wembley's 100,000 are telling all Britain about it today

APRIL FLOWERS

In a garden gay with magnolias, the latest and prettiest in swim wear is well suited to adorn the brightest and prettiest of ladies as they greet the Spring sun in suburban London. Pat Purser puts a garland of blossom round the shoulders of shapely Sheila Rathbone, her companion of the grove.

Our Writers Cover The World

Three of the "Sunday Pictorial's" team of writers are now overseas. They have been sent there to give a factual picture of various phases of international life.
★

FREDERIC MULLALLY is in France to report on the political scene. Today his candid commentary carries a Paris date line. Watch for his report on General de Gaulle's latest activities.

DICK RICHARDS has just landed in New York. He will send back news of America's stage and screen stars from Broadway and Hollywood. Turn to Page 10 for the column he cabled from the Queen Elizabeth on the way over.
★

REX NORTH, touring the Middle East at the request of our readers, is now in Greece. His report on events in that troubled land will appear in next week's "Pictorial."

The glamour of the FA Cup made front-page news in 1946 and 1947.

Sam Bartram gets to the ball before Burnley's Billy Morris in the 1947 FA Cup final, watched by Peter Croker, Harold Phipps (no. 5) and Bill Whittaker (no. 6).

The Final Countdown

The harsh winter of 1946/47 extended that first full season after the war into flaming June. Charlton finished fourth from bottom of the First Division, with FA Cup-winning hero Chris Duffy the only ever-present. Weather and war plunged the nation into economic crisis. Even footballers threatened to go on strike.

For the quarter-final, at home to the Preston of Shankly and Finney, manager Jimmy Seed was confined to his sickbed with

fever and a wireless tuned to the radio commentary. "Raymond Glendenning had me dancing around with my blankets," he said after the victory. The night before the semi-final at Elland Road, the team were stricken with food poisoning after eating salmon sandwiches on a visit to a velvet factory. Left-winger Gordon Hurst fell down a flight of hotel stairs but still played. Sam Bartram was bent double with stomach cramps during the game and Don Welsh keeled over in the dressing room afterwards. Against the odds, Charlton beat Newcastle 4-0.

The Goal that Won the Cup

The final, which took place on 26th April 1947, may have been a stinker, but it produced the most momentous goal in Charlton Athletic's history – a strike worthy of winning an FA Cup final. Chris Duffy's sweet half-volley from 14 yards hit the back of the Burnley net in the 114th minute and, in an era of polite handshakes rather than high-fives, the Addicks' match-winner galloped the length of the pitch before jumping into the arms of team-mate Jack Shreeve.

The white shirts may have been very un-Charlton, but the fact the players had socks to wear was down to full-back Peter Croker. The club had used up all their clothing coupons on Wembley tops and shorts, but luckily, Croker was friendly with a sports shop owner near his parents' home in Kingston, Surrey. An SOS – Send Our Socks – plea was answered by Umbro. Croker's mum and dad collected them on their way to Wembley on the big day.

The balding Don Welsh is unmistakable in his last Charlton team shot from 1947. Duffy is on his right. On his left is Charlie Revell, who sadly missed both FA Cup finals through injury. Keith Peacock recalls playing Sunday football in his early teenage years when Revell would turn up to watch, boots strung around his neck. If a team was short, he'd tug them on and play with rolled-up trouser legs and considerable style.

Charlie Vaughan, who scored a record 91 goals for Charlton in football's top flight, causes palpitations in the Arsenal defence on 19th November 1949, when the Addicks won at Highbury for the first time. Billy Kiernan and Gordon Hurst are the men waiting to pounce – both scored and Vaughan added the decisive goal in a 3-2 win.

1948–49 Charlton's 42 First Division matches are watched by 1,603,781 people – Valley crowds average 40,216. **11th December 1948** Charlton 4-3 Arsenal – Harold Phipps scores with a 45-yard free-kick against the reigning League Champions. And – in a reminder of the days when forwards could commit GBH on goalkeepers – Arsenal's Ian McPherson brutally bundles Bartram and ball into the net. **29th April 1950** A goal down to Derby at the Baseball Ground, with their First Division lives at stake, the Addicks players are each given a half-time glass of champagne by boss Jimmy Seed. Charlie Vaughan and Syd O'Linn score to make it 2-1 and ensure safety. **13th January 1951** Sweden international Hans Jeppson makes his Charlton debut and scores the winner in a 2-1 win over Sheffield Wednesday. **24th February 1951** Arsenal 2-5 Charlton – a hat-trick from Jeppson, whose nine goals in 11 games keep the struggling Addicks in the First Division. **18th October 1952** Charlton's Frank Lock scores from 60 yards with a free-kick in a 3-2 defeat at Newcastle. **12th September 1953** Charlton 8-1 Middlesbrough becomes the Addicks' record League victory, including an Eddie Firmani hat-trick.

Champagne & Swede Salvation

An aerial duel between Charlton defender Jock Campbell and Newcastle's Bobby 'Dazzler' Mitchell at The Valley on 10th September 1949. Mitchell won this battle, but Charlton won the match 6-3. For the second time since the Football League resumed after the war, the Addicks flirted with relegation, finishing 20th, three points above the relegation places.

In his pre-cigar and fedora days, Malcolm Allison was a bolshie 21-year-old when photographers descended on The Valley nine days before the big kick-off in August 1950. He made his only two appearances in the previous campaign. In his last interview before his death in October 2010, Big Mal was entertainingly damning about Charlton's training methods back then: "We were all standing there after one of these sessions and I said: 'Mr Trotter, the training's effing rubbish – all we do is run around the track, up and down the terracing and play 11-a-side.'

"Next morning I had to go to see Jimmy Seed, the manager, and he said: 'Malcolm, you insulted Mr Trotter yesterday.' I said: 'No I didn't, I just told him the training was rubbish.'"

Allison was soon on his way to West Ham without kicking another ball in anger for Charlton.

Pre-season training, 10th August 1950. In the centre is Charlie Vaughan, whose second successive haul of 19 goals kept the club in the top flight the season before. Vaughan was not the archetypal bulldozer no. 9 of the Nat Lofthouse era. The author, literary critic and some-time Charlton Athletic supporter David Lodge, ascribed to him: "a certain chivalric quality . . . slight in build for a centre-forward, with a beaky rather aristocratic face which usually bore an expression of amused detachment from the passions and struggles of the game swirling around him."

> " *I had come over to improve my English but Jimmy Seed got to hear about it and persuaded me to play for Charlton as an amateur.* "
>
> Hans Jeppson

Hans Jeppson (below on ball) dazzling Sheffield Wednesday on his debut for Charlton at the age of 25. The Swedish international arrived in SE7 by chance – his team back home was managed by former Charlton player Dai Astley, who had tipped off old pal Jimmy Seed when the player headed for college in England. Jeppson's flying visit went some way to keeping Charlton in the First Division in 1950–51. Of the 11 games he played, seven were won and two drawn.

There were mutterings from rivals about the unfairness of signing such a prodigious goalscoring talent and amateur who cost the club nothing. Jeppson played his last Charlton match in a 1-0 home defeat to Portsmouth and returned to Sweden with a cup as a token of the fans' appreciation. He told how after being carried shoulder high from The Valley pitch: "I was rushed over to catch the ferry back from Tilbury to Sweden as I had to conclude my studies at commercial school." He later joined Napoli for a world record £60,000.

Taking up a swathe of the 7/6 seats in the old Charlton grandstand are sailors of the Yugoslav navy, the crew of a ship which brought Marshal Tito to London for the first UK visit by a communist leader in March 1953. They were treated to a 5-1 Charlton win over Aston Villa, although clearly not everyone was transfixed. Other exotic visitors to The Valley the same year included Italian and Brazilian sailors docked at Greenwich, and the Indian ladies hockey team, who watched Charlton put six past Don Welsh's relegation-bound Liverpool on 26th September.

On 19th August 1953 five South Africans appear in the Charlton side for the 5-3 Valley mauling of a Sunderland outfit dubbed the 'Bank of England team', after costing £150,000 in transfer fees. Eddie Firmani, one of the star finds of Jimmy Seed's Cape Town trawls, is pictured scoring the first of his two goals. Fellow Springbok Stuart Leary, Cyril Hammond and Frank Lock (from the penalty spot after Leary had been brought down) were also on target.

Communal bath time at The Valley on 9th August 1954, with South African John Hewie claiming the solo tub, as Billy Kiernan, Harold Hobbis, Syd O'Linn, Stuart Leary, Eddie Firmani, Gordon Hurst, Derek Ufton and Bobby Ayre share the soap.

6th March 1954 Charlton 3-1 Portsmouth – Pompey skipper Jimmy Dickinson presents a football-pitch shaped cake to 40-year-old Sam Bartram at The Valley marking his 500th League appearance for Charlton, as British Pathé's newsreels capture the day. The Football League's later decision to discount games played in the cancelled 1939–40 season relegated the 3-1 win over Pompey to game no. 497. **25th November 1954** The minutes of the Charlton Athletic board record: "The guttering in the new stand [i.e. the Covered End, opened in 1934!] had become buckled by being continuously hit by footballs, resulting in rain water pouring on spectators during matches." The club authorize £85 for repairs. **5th February 1955** Firmani scores five in 6-1 Valley demolition of Aston Villa. **23rd April 1955** Everton 2-2 Charlton – After the match Charlton pack their muddy gear and fly to Spain where they play Alfredo Di Stéfano's Real Madrid in a friendly, losing 5-3, the season before Real launch their run of five European Cup wins. **27th December 1955** 24 hours after a 5-1 Boxing Day hammering at Old Trafford, Charlton beat the Busby Babes and League Champions elect 3-0 at The Valley; "We won the game with as brilliant display as we have ever revealed," is Seed's verdict. **10th March 1956** Charlton 2-0 Arsenal – Bartram's final match. **1st September 1956** Sunderland 8-1 Charlton is a record defeat at the time; two days later Seed is sacked after 23 years.

Highs and New Lows

Jumping to it on the eve of the 1954–55 season when Eddie Firmani, second right, scored 25 goals as a no. 10. He had played at left-back in his first match for the Addicks in 1951.

Bert Johnson played at half-back in both FA Cup finals. He scored his one and only Charlton goal in a 5-1 defeat at Huddersfield on 2nd November 1946. Most intriguingly, he was being mentored by Jimmy Seed after hanging up his boots professionally and taking a modest first step into management with nearby non-League outfit Bexleyheath and Welling. Charlton were paying his wages for a time, with the only likely explanation that he was seen as a potential successor when Seed retired. In the end, Seed was sacked, trainer Jimmy Trotter replaced him, and Bert Johnson was quietly forgotten by Charlton, although he went on to success as an assistant to Matt Gillies at Leicester City.

The team line-up for Jimmy Seed's last full season. Back row, left to right: Gordon Hurst, John Hewie, Jock Campbell, Sam Bartram, Don Townsend, Cyril Hammond, Billy Kiernan. Front row: Ken Chamberlain Bobby Ayre, Derek Ufton, Ronnie White, Jimmy Gauld. The pre-season absentee is Stuart Leary, an ever-present in that campaign, and whose 21 goals kept Charlton out of the relegation mire.

Eddie Firmani waves goodbye to England and Charlton as he boards a cross-Channel ferry in July 1955 after signing for Sampdoria. He also played for Inter and Genoa during his eight years in Italy and won three caps for the Azzurri, courtesy of qualification through his Italian grandfather. Firmani left with the goodwill of everyone at The Valley, especially the directors who trousered a £35,000 British record transfer fee. The South African star, with the football world at his feet, said: "I have nothing but wonderful memories of Charlton. It is the club that gave me the breath to breathe in soccer."

DOVER-CALAIS

The Bitter End

Jimmy Seed has the look of a man who has been stabbed in the back as he arrives home after his sacking as Charlton manager on 3rd September 1956. The directors put out the story that he resigned through ill health. Seed's love of the club made him reluctant to refute this.

He said of that day: "The football reporters took their statements, the cameras flashed. I told them of sleepless nights and of worries . . . but I could not at this stage add confusion to the official statement.

"It was one o'clock the next morning before I got to bed. September 3rd 1956 had gone on for ever. When I woke it was daylight, and, for the first seconds after regaining consciousness I wondered whether the events of yesterday were just a nightmare . . .

"I broke out in a rash all over my face and body. I had swellings on my legs and face and ran a high temperature . . . For three days and nights I was a sick man and did little else but perspire and sleep . . . it was the shock of reading about my unanticipated departure from Charlton that caused my daughter to give birth to my first grandson, James Peter Charlton Dutton."

Seed paid the ultimate price for Charlton's lack of ambition and investment – in The Valley, in players and in the future. The attitude of the directors is summed up by chairman Stanley Gliksten, who commented after Seed had been thwarted in his attempt to sign England's finest footballer: "A good job we didn't buy Matthews, it would have been money down the drain."

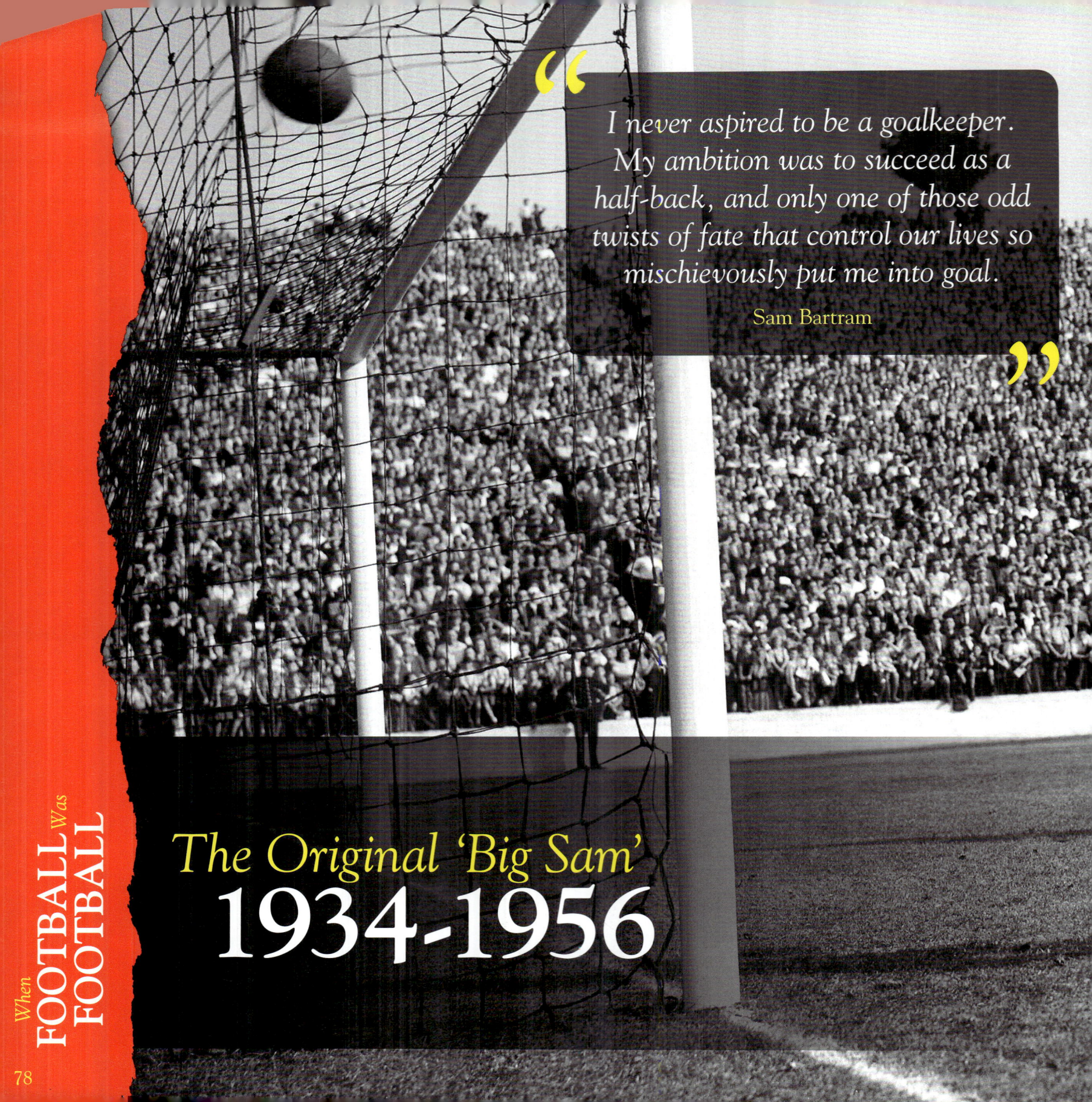

The Original 'Big Sam'
1934-1956

Two Matches in One Day

Sam Bartram, Charlton's goalkeeper, who has been bedridden with blood-poisoning, is hoping to be fit to play on Saturday, which is also his wedding day. Miss Helen Richards, the bride-to-be, is here seen with her fiancé.

Sam Bartram in his trademark cap, dark green jersey and voluminous shorts that would not have looked out of place on the mast of a Thames sailing barge. He was a Valley institution and one-club giant for more than 20 years. By common consent, he is the best goalkeeper never to have been capped by England.

Bartram acrobatics at The Valley when Charlton beat Manchester City 2-1 with goals by Stuart Leary and Benny Fenton on 5th December 1953.

'A Gymnast with Ball Skills'

That was Jimmy Seed's definition of a good goalkeeper. Occasionally Bartram's skill with the ball went to his head – he had only ended up as a goalkeeper by accident after all.

His first attempt at a football career was a failed trial as a half-back at Reading. Back playing for Boldon Villa in the North-East, he was switched to centre-forward and scored a hat-trick in his first match.

Seed's brother Anthony turned up for a local cup tie and when the Boldon keeper was injured, the tall, athletic young man with the shock of wavy red hair eagerly took over in goal. It ended 0-0 and Anthony Seed turned up for the replay for another look at this promising young keeper – except Sam was back playing wing-half!

That might have been the end of the Bartram story had it not been for Alex Wright's untimely death at Torquay in September 1934. On his brother's advice, Jimmy Seed arranged to stop off in Newcastle on the journey back from Scotland after attending Wright's funeral. Bartram borrowed half a crown from his mum for the train and met Seed in the County Hotel where the Charlton manager offered him a two-month trial – and £5 a week if he made the grade. "I swallowed hard. If I'd been offered 30 shillings a week I would have gone," said Bartram. "But five pounds!"

Three days later, on 15th September 1934, he made his debut for the reserves, who were stuffed 6-0 at Luton – The Valley's favourite son had arrived!

Three years later, he was soaking in the communal tub after a 2-1 last-day win over Brentford at The Valley – and bathing in the glory of being an ever-present as the Addicks finished second in their debut First Division season – when the shouts of "We want Bartram!" filtered through to the changing rooms.

With only a towel to protect his modesty, Sam was led to the directors' box to address his adoring public: "Thanks so . . . thanks very . . . thanks . . . it's very nice of you," was all he could say.

Bartram's Greatest Games

12th October 1935 Newcastle United 1-2 Charlton – All the goals come in the first-half and Bartram is caught on the calf by flying studs as he saves from Jim Imrie. When he untapes his socks at half-time blood spurts out of his right leg. Seven stitches later a patched-up Bartram trots out and keeps a clean sheet to secure victory. **22nd October 1938** Portsmouth 0-2 Charlton – Sam saves a penalty after George Tadman and Sailor Brown had scored for the Addicks, then he is hit by half a house brick and had his goal set alight by the Pompey fans. Not to mention standing defiant against a late Portsmouth onslaught. **26th April 1947** Burnley 0-1 Charlton – A clean sheet and an FA Cup winners' medal, the pinnacle of Sam Bartram's Charlton Athletic career. His only regret was that his mum missed his proudest moment – the losing final of the previous year had been too traumatic to risk a repeat.
7th February 1948 Manchester United 2-0 Charlton – Bartram is chaired off the pitch by both sets of players after FA Cup fifth-round defeat. Bartram called it his greatest performance: "One match, and one moment, that stood out from all the others and remained carved in my memory. No Aunt Sally at a fairground ever underwent so prolonged and furious a peppering."
26th August 1950 Blackpool 0-0 Charlton – Bartram is the hero in a thrilling goalless draw, keeping the two Stans, Matthews and Mortensen, at bay.
6th March 1954 Sam's 500th game that wasn't. On the morning of the match, the *Daily Mirror* teased: "Met a man yesterday who – honest – had NOT heard that Sam Bartram plays his 500th League match for Charlton against Portsmouth today!" Lost amid the cake presentations and celebrations, was the fact that the veteran Charlton keeper played an absolute blinder – the *Sunday Pictorial* reported: "Half a dozen saves in the first-half must have been some of his greatest ever."

LEFT: Training at The Valley in January 1951. The man remains such an icon that this image can be seen on amazon.co.uk adorning a Sam Bartram phone sock "fitting any iPhone or Blackberry" for £5.99 – just a little more than Sam was earning a week in his first days at Charlton.

BELOW: Sam on his backside as Newcastle put the skids under Charlton who are thrashed 6-0 at St James' Park on 26th January 1952. Frank Lock on the goal-line and no. 6 Cyril Hammond deny Jackie Milburn this time, as no. 2 John Hewie takes a snow bath.

84

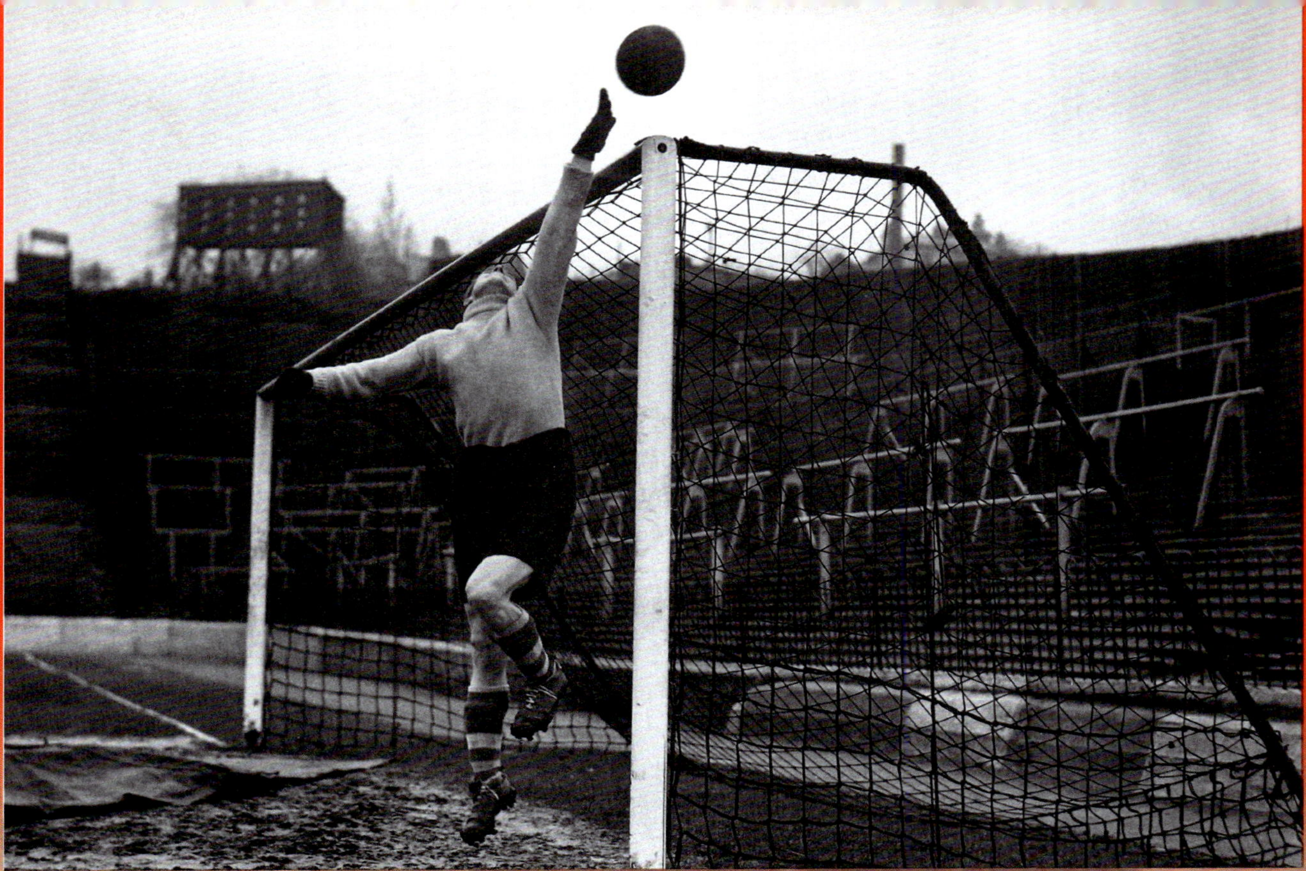

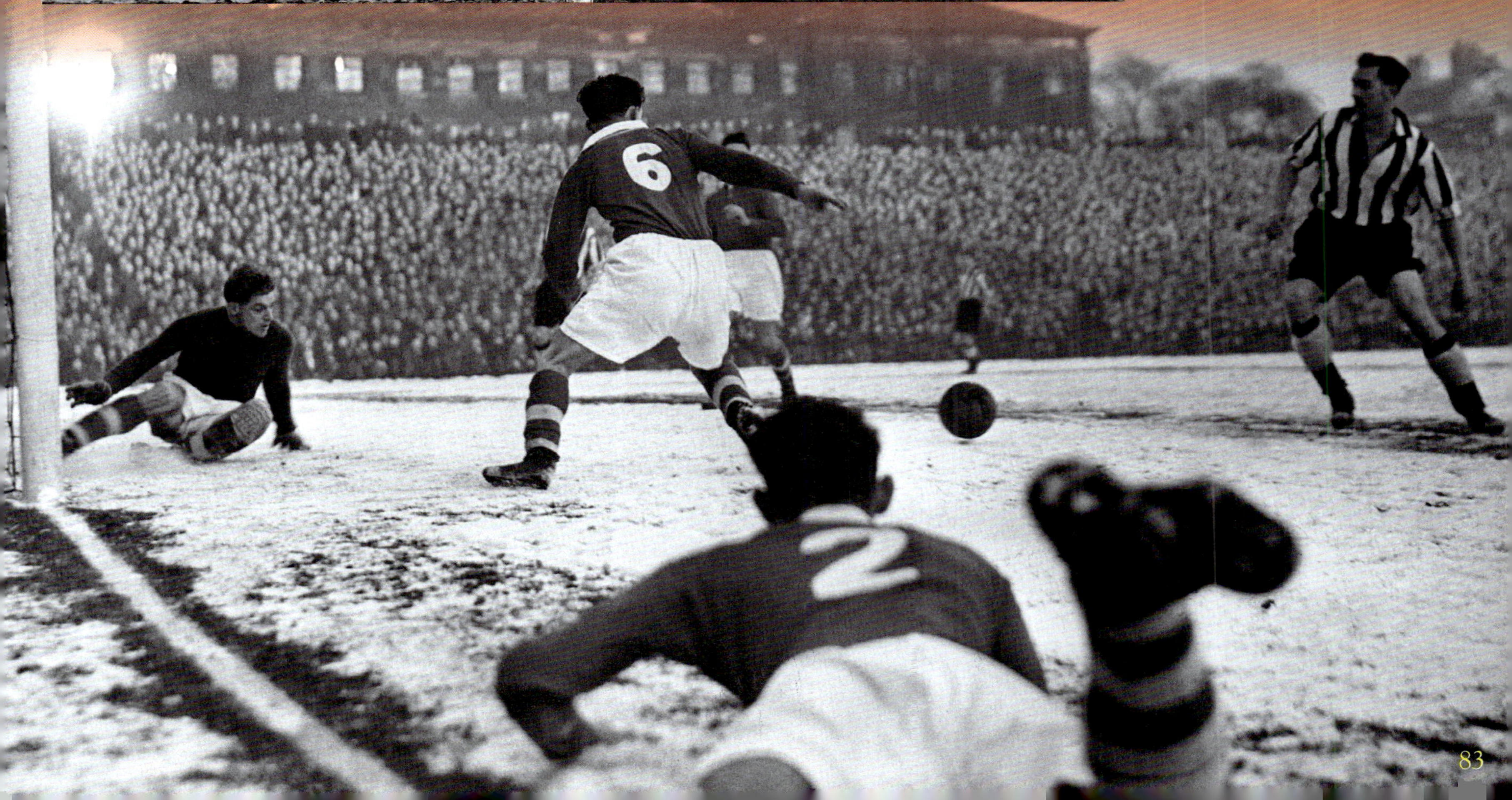

83

The Bartram mantra was "practise, practise, practise and still more practise". Note the bare hands, although Sam did recommend gloves in wet weather for any budding net-minder, declaring: "I have found that there is only one kind of glove which is of any use, and this is the woollen type; the wool clings to your hand, thus allowing you to get a good grip." But he was not averse to

innovation – his daredevil antics made him the perfect guinea pig when a crash-hat was developed after a series of bad injuries. But Sam stuck with his trusty cap, rain or shine: "It prevents the rain-drops from trickling down the forehead and into the eyes," said the man remembered for occasionally charging out of the area, whipping off his peaked cap and heading clear.

Football was not going to last forever, so Sam Bartram started thinking of his future and opened his own sports shop around the corner from The Valley, with a sideline in print and stationery. This was before the days of club superstores and replica shirts with players' names at £1 per iron-on letter – what a killing he'd have made on Albert Uytenbogaardt merchandise! The shop was still there in the 1960s, long after Sam had retired and gone into management. One youngster who used to help out was Brian Kinsey, who became another great servant of Charlton, playing almost 400 games.

You've got to pity the poor kid in those boots Sam is trying on him for size (right). Matt Busby Championships, Arthur Rowe 6.5s, the Stubert Walley Barnes popular boot – even back then they had the star-name branding, but they were almost universally heel-skinning, toe-curling clodhoppers.

BELOW: With Bartram out injured, South African Albert Uytenbogaardt makes his debut in a 4-1 home win against Stoke on 18th December 1948. The keeper, christened 'Humphrey Bogart' by the fans, made only five more League appearances over the next five years. Charlton lost just once when Bogie was in goal – an 8-4 pasting at Blackpool on 27th September 1952 – which was also his last game for the club.

Sam's Final Bow

It started with a 2-0 defeat in a Division Three (South) scrap at Watford and ended almost 22 years later at The Valley with the 2-0 victory over Arsenal in 1956. Young and old dashed on to the pitch at the final whistle to shake the hand of the Charlton legend. At the age of 42, Sam Bartram had played his last game and, just as in 1937, this modest hero had to grab a towel and be dragged from the changing rooms to say an emotional farewell to the thousands chanting his name.

Bartram never did win the international cap he might have cherished as much as his FA Cup winners' medal. He did, though, play in Possibles v Probables and England 3 matches and toured Australia with FA representative sides. The Australia trip, at the end of a long, hard 1950–51 season, was a 21-match epic.

He was runner-up to Tom Finney in the Football Writers' Footballer of the Year award for 1954. Jimmy Seed told the *Daily Mirror*: "I shall feel a big wrench when I pin up the team for next week's match without Sam's name at the top. You don't find another Sam Bartram without a long, long search."

BELOW: Sam and family leave The Valley for the last time.

Bartram and Firmani in reflective mood on 18th July 1955 – the two Charlton legends were soon to go their separate ways, Eddie off to Italy and Sam into retirement the following year. With Jimmy Seed's days at The Valley also numbered, a watershed moment in the club's history was approaching.

Bartram went straight into management at York City, for whom he had turned out during the war, scoring two penalties in one match. He never seems to have been considered by Charlton when Seed was given the bullet. After a spell in charge of Luton he left to become a football reporter with the *Sunday People*. The late sports editor Neville Holtham used to rib Sam about running around as if he were still a super-fit athlete, encouraging him to take a cab instead of slogging uphill to his house in Harpenden every evening. Sam died on 17th July 1981 while on his way home from the office. He was 67.

In the decades since his passing, Sam Bartram still stands almost 10ft tall at The Valley, his smiling statue a magnet for every camera phone.

"

When for the last time he took the goalkeeper's gloves from his gnarled hands – rough-hewn in the service of Charlton – and hung up his worn and dilapidated cap, it gave me cause for reflection. I remembered his loyalty. No more faithful, constant and true-hearted man has played the game of football.

Jimmy Seed in his preface to Sam Bartram's autobiography

"

Relegation, 7-6 & Golden Summers
1956-1960

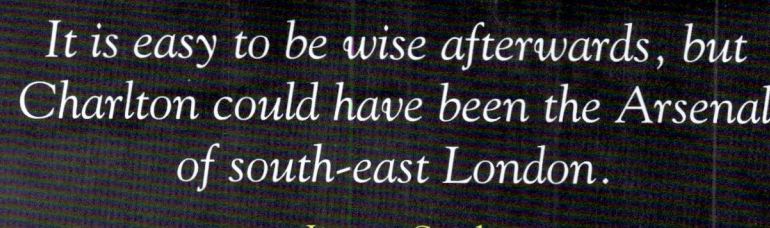

> **It is easy to be wise afterwards, but Charlton could have been the Arsenal of south-east London.**
>
> Jimmy Seed

Charlton players larking in the snow on a training break to Eastbourne on 21st January 1958, during the club's gripping but ultimately heartbreaking first season back in the second tier for 21 years.

Decline and Fall

The decline had been going on for years, so the fall was no great surprise. Charlton dropped back into the Second Division. A pall of desolation hung over The Valley during that 1956–57 relegation season. A few years after averaging crowds of 40,000, attendances had halved. The crowd for Aston Villa on 15th December 1956, when this picture was taken, was 13,452 – a far cry from February 1938 when 75,000 had watched the two sides in the FA Cup.

Bartram was gone and Seed had also gone by the time Villa came to The Valley. The fabric of the club seemed to be disintegrating. Even 'the Addicks' nickname had been supplanted by 'the Robins' and bandleader Billy Cotton enriched football's dubious musical heritage and everlasting Charlton tradition with his version of the 'When the Red, Red Robin' – a ditty made famous by a 1955 Susan Hayward weepie called *I'll Cry Tomorrow*.

The first game of 1956, a 3-1 loss at Villa Park, had Jimmy Seed contemplating a doomsday scenario a fortnight before he was fired: "No spirit or fight. No team-work. The Red is Shining!" was his ominous verdict.

New manager Jimmy Trotter (below) could not stop the rot, despite the arrival of two talented new frontmen, Johnny Summers and Sam Lawrie. With the game up and Charlton down, the directors delivered a smug appraisal as the Division One glory days lurched to an ignominious end. The club finished bottom, 10 points from safety, and the programme notes for the last home match recorded: "While we share with our supporters the natural disappointment at the loss of Division One status, those guiding the destinies of the club have long since dried their eyes . . . the policy of giving Charlton's young players their big chance is the most likely to restore the club to its rightful place. It is a policy which should have been pursued years ago, when sentiment was allowed to override good judgement."

Fool's Gauld

Charlton inside-right Jimmy Gauld (below left) playing against Everton in September 1956. Gauld was plucked from League of Ireland football to take over the goalscoring mantle from Eddie Firmani. He scored both the goals when Charlton beat Arsenal in Sam Bartram's final game in March 1956 and looked good value for his £4,000 fee with a return of 21 goals in 47 appearances.

But a quarter of the way into the following relegation season he was allowed to leave for Everton for £10,500.

The Scottish inside-forward scored seven in 23 games for the Toffees and had successful spells at Plymouth and Swindon before drifting into the backwaters of St Johnstone and Mansfield, where a broken leg ended his career.

And that might have been the last anybody ever heard of Jimmy Gauld if he had not taken up a new vocation of fixing football matches. In 1964 he was jailed for four years for a betting scandal that also put two England internationals – Tony Kay and Peter Swan – and Sheffield Wednesday team-mate David 'Bronco' Layne behind bars. All were banned for life from even watching football – though the disgraced Swan and Layne had their ban lifted in 1972.

Mr Justice Lawton branded Gauld "responsible for the ruin of footballers of distinction," adding: "It is clear that over a long period of three years from one end of this kingdom to another you have befouled professional soccer and corrupted your friends and acquaintances."

Seed may no longer have been Charlton's cup
but he was back in South London less than two
as manager of Third Division Millwall. Here
assistant Ron Gray. Arriving at The Den,
unced: "I aim to put spirit and confidence
side." A Millwall historian records: "In fact
has, before or since, ever made a worse
reer at Millwall." They finished 23rd and
the new Division Four. Seed handed over
emained a director of the club until his
ly 1966, aged 71.

Back to Division Two

8th September 1956 Charlton 4-4 Sheffield Wednesday – Following the departure of Seed, club director David Clark is put in charge. After losing their first five matches, Charlton trail 3-1 at the interval. Billy Kiernan pulls another goal back, but Wednesday score again to go 4-2 up. South Africans Stuart Leary and John Hewie, however, both hit the target to earn Charlton their first point of the season. **12th September 1956** Trainer Jimmy Trotter is appointed the fifth manager in Charlton's history and they lose 2-0 at Bolton. **10th November 1956** Charlton 0-2 Cardiff – The Addicks hit the woodwork six times, but can't get on the scoresheet. **16th November 1956** Charlton sign Johnny Summers from Millwall and Sam Lawrie from Middlesbrough for a combined sum of £7,800. **13th April 1957** Charlton 1-2 Burnley – the beaten FA Cup finalists of 10 years earlier condemn Charlton to relegation with four games to play. **21st December 1957** Charlton 7-6 Huddersfield Town – 10-man Charlton are 5-1 down with less than half an hour left, but Summers hits five and Huddersfield become the only team to score six goals and lose a League match. **26th April 1958** Needing a point at home to Blackburn to bounce straight back to the top flight, Charlton lose 4-3 and Rovers are promoted instead. **14th November 1959** Charlton are humiliated 11-1 at Aston Villa, using three goalkeepers in the process. Willie Duff lets in six before going off with a dislocated finger. He is replaced by full-back Don Townsend, who concedes three. Then striker Stuart Leary takes over between the sticks and lets in two more. **2nd April 1960** In the return match at The Valley against the soon-to-be crowned Second Division Champions, Villa are beaten 2-0 with goals from Lawrie and Summers. **22nd October 1960** Three weeks after a 7-4 thrashing of Pompey (five Summers goals again), Charlton draw 6-6 at home with Middlesbrough. Summers equalizes in the 89th minute after Brian Clough's hat-trick for Boro.

Charlton 1-5 Manchester United, 18th February 1957. Bobby Charlton rises above United team-mate Liam Whelan and Addicks keeper Willie Duff on his way to a first hat-trick in League football. John Hewie (left) and Trevor Edwards look on. Bobby had also scored two against Charlton on his United debut in the previous October.

Johnny Summers and Derek Ufton put on a relaxed pre-season training show for the cameras, 15th August 1957. Club captain Ufton (inset) gives some impromptu coaching to local boys in a ragbag of football togs – at least the socks look as if they might favour the Addicks! Meanwhile, Summers practises his shooting. He usually played inside- or outside-left so naturally favoured his left foot, which might be why he is working on that weaker right peg on the training ground. It was dedication that would pay off when Huddersfield Town came to The Valley that season and Ufton and Summers played pivotal roles in the greatest Football League comeback.

Where were the photographers when 30-year-old Johnny Summers scored the goals that briefly transformed him into the most talked-about player in English football? Certainly not at The Valley. The papers were reduced to taking pictures of Charlton's hero as he put up the decorations Chez Summers in Lewisham, watched by wife Betty and Johnny Jr., and at the Arrows pub off London's Old Kent Road.

The 13-Goal Christmas Epic

No Charlton Athletic supporter needs a refresher about the most astonishing match to be played on these shores. Christmas shopping rather than football was on most minds on 21st December 1957. A Second Division fixture against Huddersfield Town attracted a crowd of just 12,535.

Huddersfield manager Bill Shankly revved up his side by telling them: "Charlton? They're not fit to be on the same park." Charlton captain Derek Ufton went off early on with a dislocated shoulder – an injury he was to suffer no fewer than 20 times during his career. Reduced to 10 men, the Addicks were two goals down by half-time.

After a quick change of boots, Summers pulled a goal back straight after the break. But Christmas shopping began to appeal to more of The Valley faithful who headed for the exits when Huddersfield went 5-1 up. The lucky ones backtracked as a roar signalled that Charlton had made it 2-5. John 'Buck' Ryan, a rangy Scottish forward with an enviable and often overlooked goal record (10 from 19 that season), was the scorer.

A minute later Summers struck again and it was 3-5. Boss Jimmy Trotter was happy to take some credit for the jaw-dropping miracle that would unfold over the final quarter of an hour or so, saying afterwards: "Things had not been coming off for Summers, so I moved him from inside-left to centre-forward. As a last resort I switched him to outside-left."

Summers banged in an eight-minute hat-trick and the 10 men were leading 6-5 with four minutes left. There was more drama than the entire 18 years of *Armchair Theatre* that had Britain glued to its black and white TV sets in those days. And it wasn't over.

John Hewie put through his own net – generously credited to Howard of Huddersfield in the dizzy final reckoning – to make it 6-6 before Charlton went up the other end and Buck Ryan smashed in a last-gasp winner.

After seeing his side score six and lose, Shankly didn't speak to anyone for a week. Summers, with a poignancy that would only become apparent later, said: "I'll keep these boots for the rest of my life." Just five years later he died from leukaemia.

That practice session comes back to mind – all five of his goals came from his supposedly unfavoured right foot. And two crosses with his left made both of Buck Ryan's.

Blackburn's Tom Johnston is sent sprawling by Charlton goalie Willie Duff. No. 5 Derek Ufton and John Hewie (right) are the Charlton defenders. England winger Bryan Douglas scores from the spot – and effectively condemns Charlton fans to 40 years of hurt. It was to be that long before top-flight football returned to The Valley.

The Valley of Tears

If 21st December 1957 was one of the most memorable days in the annals of Charlton Athletic, then 26th April 1958 is one of the saddest. As the 1957–58 season drew to a dramatic finale, Charlton were on the brink of an instant return to the First Division. The battle for promotion had see-sawed between the Addicks, West Ham United, Liverpool, Fulham and Blackburn Rovers.

Charlton went into the last game of the season in blistering form after a 5-1 away demolition of Rotherham, a 4-1 home win over Notts County and a 4-1 stuffing of Ipswich Town at Portman Road. A point at home to Blackburn would seal promotion.

Charlton had looked unstoppable with Johnny Summers a devastating ever-present, scoring 28 goals.

Blackburn had tricky winger Bryan Douglas, who was filling Stanley Matthews' boots in the England team. Ally McLeod, of 'Ally's Army' 1978 World Cup notoriety, played left-wing.

The critical moment of the game came just after Freddie Lucas had nodded the Addicks into a fourth-minute lead. Stuart Leary was clean through but his attempt to nutmeg keeper Leyland was easily saved.

Peter Dobing's two goals and one from Roy Vernon put Rovers 3-1 up at half-time. Duff's rash challenge on centre-forward Johnston allowed Douglas to make it 4-1 from the spot in the 62nd minute.

But the record Second Division crowd of 56,435 must have had visions of the 7-6 Christmas cracker when Eddie Firmani's younger brother, Peter, made it 4-2 with less than 15 minutes to go. John Hewie clawed another one back with an 83rd-minute penalty after Leary was upended in the box, but despite battering Blackburn for the final desperate minutes, the equalizer and the point that might have changed the entire course of Charlton Athletic history, never came.

Grown men wept that day, not for the first time or the last. Youngsters whose feet would hardly touch the ground in the throng till they reached Charlton Church Lane were inconsolable. Perhaps they had premonitions of the dark years of decline to come.

Right-winger Eddie Werge is sent flying in the penalty area in the Blackburn promotion decider. 50,000-plus Charlton fans hold their breath, but the referee waves play on.

LEGENDS

Johnny Summers

Summers' Day

Johnny Summers heads Charlton in front two minutes into the 2-1 victory over Cardiff at Ninian Park on 31st March 1959. It was the Addicks' third game in three days over Easter – they drew 0-0 with Cardiff at The Valley the previous day, Easter Monday, and lost 2-1 at Stoke on the Saturday.

FOOTBALL –STATS–

Johnny Summers

Name: Johnny Summers

Born: Shepherds Bush, 10th September 1927

Died: London, 2nd June 1962, aged 34

Position: Forward

Charlton career: 1956–61

Appearances: 182

Other clubs: Fulham, Norwich, Millwall

Goals: 104

His five-goal haul against Huddersfield tends to overshadow his marvellous Charlton record. Sadly he arrived too late to save Jimmy Seed's job and Charlton's place at football's highest table.

When
FOOTBALL *Was* FOOTBALL

The Elephant in the Gloom
1961-1969

> *It's just like getting out of jail.*
>
> Jimmy Trotter after being sacked in November 1961

Nellie the baby elephant entertains The Valley crowd before Charlton played Portsmouth on 4th October 1969. Bemused fans were also treated to the sight of a camel parading around the ground, but unfortunately there were no new marquee signings to be afforded the same honour.

Re-christened the Valley of Doom or Valley of Death, this was the depressing, rain-sodden scene in November 1961, with Charlton bottom of the Second Division.

Michael Gliksten in the gothic splendour of the oak-panelled boardroom at The Valley after succeeding his father Stanley as Charlton Athletic chairman in 1962 at the age of 23 – a position he held for 20 years. He liked to be addressed as 'Mr Michael'. The Valley as a place where time stood still is borne out by season ticket prices in 1965–66 – 8 guineas, 6 guineas or 3 guineas, a coinage last seen when it was used to pay the Duke of Wellington's army in the Pyrenees. The Gliksten family bought the club in 1932 and sold it in 1982 to Mark Hulyer. If fans thought the 1960s were grim, they were nothing compared to the traumas to come in the 1980s.

October 1961 With Charlton bottom of the Second Division, Jimmy Trotter is sacked after five years and director David Clark takes over, as he had done when Jimmy Seed left. Frank Hill, a Scot who played in the great Herbert Chapman Arsenal side of the 1930s, is put in charge in November and leads Charlton to safety. **26th September 1962** League Cup second round, Leicester 4-4 Charlton – The First Division side go 4-0 up after 37 minutes. Keith Peacock, who signed professional forms for Charlton in July 1962, scores twice between Brian Kinsey and Fred Lucas strikes to make it 4-4. The Addicks win The Valley replay 2-1 before going out at Fourth Division Leyton Orient in the fourth round. **24th May 1963** 18-year-old Peacock scores as Charlton win 2-1 against Walsall at Fellows Park and avoid dropping to the third tier of English football for the first time since the 1930s. **5th October 1963** Eddie Firmani returns from Italy and scores twice in a 3-1 win at Manchester City. **August 1965** Bob Stokoe is appointed manager after Hill's dismissal. **21st August 1965** Bolton 4-2 Charlton. Addicks keeper Mick Rose goes off injured after 11 minutes, John Hewie takes over in goal and Peacock becomes the first Football League substitute. **September 1967** Stokoe goes and Eddie Firmani – that season's leading scorer – moves from the pitch to the manager's chair at The Valley. **7th September 1968** Charlton 2-1 Portsmouth – South London neighbours Charlton, Millwall and Crystal Palace briefly stand at one, two and three in Division Two. Derby end up Champions, Palace runners-up and Charlton miss out on promotion, finishing third. **16th November 1968** The *Match of the Day* cameras make their first visit to The Valley for a 1-1 draw with Hull City.

Returning Hero

Twelve years after first setting foot in The Valley, Eddie Firmani shows son Paul where it all started, while on a visit to his in-laws at nearby Catford, 8th November 1962.

Eight years after waving farewell from the gangplank of a cross-Channel ferry, Eddie Firmani is back to revive Charlton's fortunes. The club were still in Division Two, thanks to a 2-1 last-day win the previous season away to Walsall, who played half the game without a recognized goalkeeper. Firmani, who amazingly turned down Lazio to return to The Valley, is pictured scoring against Manchester City at Maine Road in his first comeback game. He added a second in the 3-1 win.

Whenever Michael Gliksten (or Charlton) needed someone to save them from relegation, they used to say he always sent for Eddie Firmani. Charlton were third bottom. They needed me and I was happy to help out.

– Eddie Firmani

–LEGENDS–

Stuart Leary

Stuart Leary is a worthy candidate for finest player to wear the Charlton shirt. As an all-round sportsman the South African had few equals. A Kent cricketer of distinction, Leary tends to be overshadowed by Firmani and Summers in Charlton folklore of the era.

He remains the club's record League marksman with 153. The 13 goals he scored in the 1961–62 season, last of his 11 at The Valley, tell only part of the story. Charlton were bottom on nine points with almost half the season gone when Leary – Hans Jeppson-style – single-handedly hauled them to Second Division safety.

Leary played for England at under-23 level alongside 'Busby Babe' Duncan Edwards, but was barred from the full national side because of rules demanding players had to have an English father. He still, however, had to do National Service for the country that had blackballed him as a footballer.

Leary's 403-game Charlton career came to a wretched end when he fell out with manager Frank Hill after returning late from a trip home and he was sold to QPR for £17,000.

His cricketing career – Charlton's Derek Ufton and Syd O'Linn were Kent team-mates – continued into the early 1970s. O'Linn hailed Leary as the cleverest footballer he knew. Colin Cowdrey, Charlton director and Kent cricket captain, likened him to George Best many years later.

Leary was found dead on Table Mountain, Cape Town, on 23rd August 1988, having been missing for five days. He was just 55.

Stuart Leary (left) on his way out to field for Kent against Warwickshire with Colin Cowdrey (right) on 30th August 1967.

FOOTBALL
–STATS–

Stuart Leary

Name: Stuart Leary

Born: Cape Town, South Africa, 30th April 1933

Died: Cape Town, 23rd August 1988, aged 55

Position: Forward

Charlton career: 1951–62

Appearances: 403

Goals: 163

Other clubs: QPR, Kent CCC

Leary's tragic end remains a mystery, along with how Charlton could possibly have let such a great player go when all he needed was a break from relentless football and cricket.

ABOVE: Leary after arriving home in Bexleyheath from South Africa on 23rd November 1962. His late return caused a major falling-out with manager Frank Hill. Leary got as far as training back at The Valley (right), but never played for Charlton Athletic again.

Two of the greatest exports of 1950s English football back in the fold and going head to head at The Valley in their Division Two twilight years. Cardiff's John Charles fails to stop Eddie Firmani scoring Charlton's first in a 5-2 caning of Cardiff at The Valley on 26th October 1963. The pair had clashed many times in Italy where Charles played for Juventus and Roma during Firmani's time in Serie A with Sampdoria, Inter and Genoa.

Brian Kinsey was the backflip king as well as being Sam Bartram's shop boy. Kinsey's Charlton pedigree stretched back to the days when his grandfather helped dig out The Valley from the wasteland of the Charlton Sandpits. And he was even brought into the world by the long-serving club physician, a Dr Montgomery. Kinsey's 14 seasons and 411 games earned him this glowing tribute in his testimonial programme of 25th April 1969: "Perhaps the top honours have eluded him but the character and dedication he has shown in 12 years as a Charlton professional are worth more than all the cups and medals football could have given him."

Billy Bonds, a Charlton and West Ham legend, jumping for the ball with Cliff Myers and Ray Keeley in August 1964.

—LEGENDS—

Mike Bailey

Mike Bailey made his name with Charlton, playing for England under-21s and winning his two caps for the full international side while still at The Valley. He suffered a horrific double fracture of his left leg in a fourth-round FA Cup replay at Middlesbrough in February 1964, but he was back the following season.

Wolverhampton Wanderers came knocking in February 1966 and one of the finest wing-halves in the country was gone. Bailey returned to The Valley as manager in 1980 and guided the club to promotion from Division Three. He left for Brighton before they played a match back in the second tier.

FOOTBALL —STATS—

Mike Bailey

Name: Mike Bailey

Born: Wisbech, 27th February 1942

Position: Wing-half

Charlton career: 1960–66

Appearances: 169

Goals: 22

Other clubs: Wolves, Minnesota Kicks, Hereford United

Bailey played for Wolves in the 1972 UEFA Cup final, which they lost 3-2 on aggregate to Tottenham Hotspur.

Mike Bailey returns home
after breaking his leg in two
places at Ayresome Park.

August 1965, Bob Stokoe's first season in charge and some fine players – Lenny Glover was sold to Leicester for £80,000, Mike Bailey to Wolves for £35,000 and Billy Bonds to West Ham for £50,000. Mike Kenning went to Norwich for £27,000 in December 1966, three days after scoring twice at The Valley against Ipswich. Back row, left to right: Keith Peacock, Billy Bonds, John Snedden, Ken Jones, John Hewie, Mick Rose, Brian Tocknell, Frank Haydock, Jack Kennedy. Front row: Roy Matthews, Lenny Glover, Mike Bailey, Brian Kinsey, Mike Kenning.

Tocknell recalled the gruelling regime under coach Dick Graham during Stokoe's reign: "Dick was the sort of guy who used to like players running up and down terraces with backpacks filled with bricks. It was more like commando training than anything to do with football."

This puss was adopted by Charlton and christened 'Lucky' after straying into The Valley in August 1968. Charlton did not lose another match until the end of September and went on to finish third in the Second Division, their highest position for 11 years.

Lucky's influence showed up in the FA Cup as well. Two stirring third-round ties against Crystal Palace brought the crowds back. After a 0-0 at The Valley, Charlton went to Selhurst Park and won 2-0 in front of just short of 40,000 people.

The reward was a fourth-round tie against Arsenal, rekindling memories of the days when the clubs met regularly at the highest level. The Gunners won 2-0 in front of 55,760 at Highbury.

Lucky's last significant act was to relieve himself on the pitch during a League match against Derby. Ronnie Moore went on to score the only goal of the game in the 84th minute.

Charlton goalkeeper Charlie Wright looks the happiest man at Selhurst Park after Ray Treacy's killer second goal in the FA Cup replay against Crystal Palace, 8th January 1969.

Five days before the drawn FA Cup tie against Crystal Palace at The Valley, Charlie Wright is out directing ice-breaking operations. Brian Kinsey (right) and Keith Peacock are wielding the forks, 31st December 1968.

–LEGENDS–

Bob Curtis

Bob Curtis, drafted into the side as a teenager after Billy Bonds left for West Ham, toasts his 19th birthday, which fell on 25th January 1969, the day of the FA Cup fourth-round tie at Arsenal. He was a terrace hero for more than 10 seasons, famed for the outrageous blond mop that he'd dyed as a tribute to his hero Bobby Moore, his braveheart commitment and scorching penalty kicks.

FOOTBALL –STATS–

Bob Curtis

Name: Bob Curtis

Born: Langwith, Nottinghamshire, 25th January 1950

Died: 19th March 2010, aged 60

Position: Right-back; midfield

Charlton career: 1966–78

Appearances: 358

Goals: 37

Other clubs: Mansfield Town, Kettering Town

Curtis scored a record 20 penalties for Charlton so he's forgiven the last-day miss against Preston in April 1975 – the Addicks still won 3-1 to return to Division Two. He died in 2010 following a long battle with motor neurone disease.

Bob Curtis in Superman mode as he tries to stop QPR scoring in a 3-3 draw at The Valley, 3rd February 1968.

AEROSIGNS

Charlton were back in a relegation battle in 1969–70 and finished 20th. Gates at The Valley plummeted and Firmani paid with his job. Back row, left to right: Tony Burns, Bob Curtis, John Keirs, Matt Tees, Charlie Wright. Middle row: Dennis Booth, Peter Reeves, Paul Went, Graham Moore, Jack Burkett, Brian Kinsey, Harry Gregory. Front row: Ray Crawford, Alan Campbell, Eddie Firmani, Keith Peacock, Ray Treacy.

One newcomer was Luciano Masiello, a Naples-born forward who grew up in Lewisham and went to St Austin RC Boys' School in Charlton. The *Daily Mirror* considered an Italian playing in England exotic enough to pay a house visit on the eve of Masiello's debut against Norwich at The Valley in December 1969. Charlton won 3-0. The Italian South Londoner made eight appearances in total, six of them in the League. His only goal came in a 3-1 second-round League Cup defeat at The Hawthorns against West Bromwich Albion in September 1970, the last time he pulled on a Charlton shirt.

When FOOTBALL Was FOOTBALL

The Killer Seventies
1970-1979

> *It was just one of those things.*
>
> Derek Hales, when quizzed about his infamous punch-up with team-mate Mike Flanagan

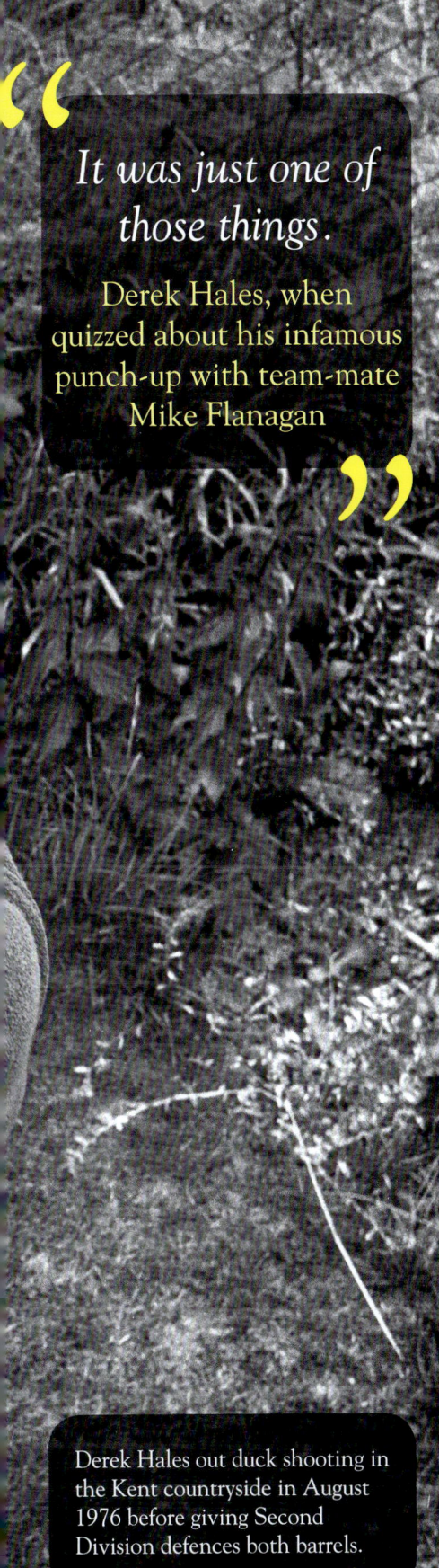

Derek Hales out duck shooting in the Kent countryside in August 1976 before giving Second Division defences both barrels.

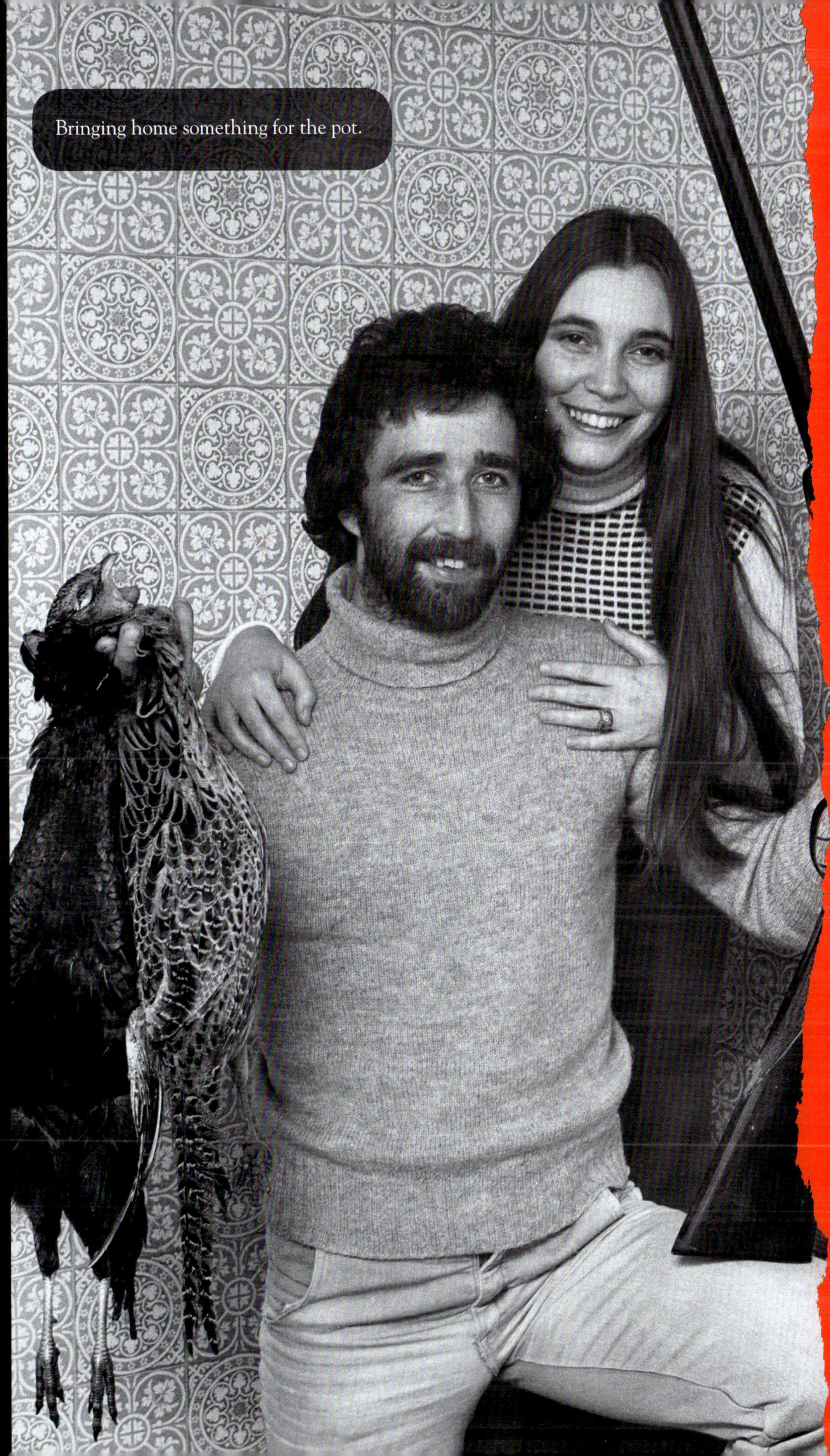

Bringing home something for the pot.

Manager-Go-Round

30th March 1970 Eddie Firmani is fired and Theo Foley takes over as manager. **29th April 1972** Charlton lose 5-0 at Bob Stokoe's Blackpool and are condemned to the Third Division for the first time since 1935. **28th November 1972** At Charlton's 2-1 home win over Brentford, the fans are asked to sign a petition supporting a new Valley sports complex "on the lines of Moscow Dynamo, Real Madrid and Benfica". **1972–73** Arthur Horsfield scores 29 goals and is player of the year. **23rd July 1973** Derek Hales arrives from Luton on a three-month trial. **1973–74** Average attendances sink to 5,306, worse than every other London club except Brentford and Charlton's poorest ever. **16th March 1974** Just 850 watch Charlton at Rochdale in Division Three. **20th April 1974** Theo Foley is presented with a rose bowl to mark his four years in charge before the home game with Watford. Charlton lose 3-1 and Foley is sacked three days later. **17th May 1974** Andy Nelson, a Football League Champion in his Ipswich playing days, becomes the third Charlton manager in four years.

Charlton 2-0 Bristol City. Debut boy Eamonn Rogers racing City's Trevor Tainton for the ball in the match on 30th October 1971. Rogers was an Eire international forward but failed to have the impact of Foley's other signings Derek Hales, Mick Flanagan and Colin Powell.

Not much changed at The Valley – the same bench seat used for years, if not decades, in the obligatory pre-season training shot was wheeled out again in July 1971 for Derek Bellotti, Paul Went, Bob Curtis, Peter Reeves and Keith Peacock to hurdle.

Charlton celebrate after securing the third Division Three promotion
spot with a 3-1 home victory over Preston in front of nearly 25,000 fans
at The Valley, 29th April 1975.

Team of All the Attacking Talents

Theo Foley laid the groundwork for Charlton's enjoyable resurgence in the mid-1970s. He brought in four of the most exciting players seen at the club for many a year. Arthur Horsfield, Mike Flanagan, Derek Hales and Colin Powell combined with the guile and experience of veteran Keith Peacock to drag Charlton out of their Third Division pit and double gates along the way.

Horsfield had been a makeweight in the sale of Ray Treacy to Swindon in June 1972. He played 156 consecutive matches, scoring 61 goals and dropping back to make a rock-solid centre-half in the 1974–75 promotion campaign.

Foley, as a match-day host at The Valley, was still singing the praises of Flanagan in the 2013–14 season and marvelling at how he managed to nab him from Tottenham.

Hales cost just £4,000 from Luton. Wing wizard Colin Powell was talent-spotted by Charlton as a teenager – it was another seven years before he arrived at The Valley from Barnet in January 1973 for £10,000.

Foley was not around long enough to enjoy the fruits of his shrewd dealings, as Andy Nelson oversaw the return to Division Two.

And the Charlton man voted fans' player of the season in that 1974-75 promotion campaign? Not Horsfield, Powell, Peacock or 20-goal Hales, but home-grown blond midfield battler Richie Bowman (pictured).

The Charlton Athletic squad for the 1975–76 season. Arthur Horsfield was on his way to Watford by the time this team shot left the darkroom. Back row, left to right: Les Berry, Jimmy Giles, Graham Tutt, Colin Powell, Bob Goldthorpe. Middle row: Arthur Horsfield, Bob Curtis, George Hope, Mark Penfold, Harry Cripps, Richie Bowman, Mike Flanagan, Ray Tumbridge. Front row: Phil Warman, Peter Hunt, David Young, Derek Hales, Keith Peacock.

ABOVE: Teenager Graham Tutt – a goalkeeper of huge promise.

RIGHT: Jim Giles jumping with Ian Porterfield of Sunderland in a 2-1 defeat on 15th November 1975. The match was watched by Jimmy Trotter, back at The Valley for the first time since his 1961 sacking.

139

LEFT: The Who's wildman drummer Keith Moon pours vodka over Aussie actor and comedian Garry McDonald before The Valley gig after taking umbrage at being ambushed for a spoof interview.

RIGHT: The Who playing the loudest ever rock concert in front of 76,000 fans at The Valley on 31st May 1976. Even more had watched the same band there two years earlier.

"*We were basically being crushed for several minutes – a human logjam, with way too many people in a confined space. Close to panic. You read about the various tragedies at places like Cincinnati (The Who again), and all the English soccer disasters, and you realize that it could quite easily have happened at Charlton.*"

Who fan identified only as 'Jonathan' on www.ukrockfestivals.com

Graham Tutt pictured in July 1975. At the age of 18, the local lad had established himself as the Addicks' first-choice goalie, making 30 appearances in the 1974–75 promotion run. On 21st February 1976, Tutt was kicked in the face by Tommy Finney of Sunderland seven minutes into a match at Roker Park. His nose was broken and the horrific injuries to his right eye meant he would never play League football again.

–LEGENDS–

Colin Powell

FOOTBALL –STATS–

Colin Powell

Name: Colin Powell

Born: Hendon, 7th July 1948

Position: Winger

Charlton career: 1973–81

Appearances: 338

Goals: 35

Other clubs: Stevenage, Barnet, New England Tea Men, Gillingham

Hales, Horsfield and Flanagan were fantastic finishers, but 'Paddy' Powell often handed it to them on a plate.

13th December 1976 Derek Hales sold to Derby for £333,333. **8th May 1977** Hales receives the goal of the season award from ITV for his second strike of a hat-trick in a 3-1 win over Hull at The Valley on 9th October the previous year. **3rd May 1978** Another relegation nail-biter. Charlton had let Colin Powell and Mike Flanagan join US side New England Tea Men, thinking they were safe. It ends 0-0 and Charlton survive. **27th July 1978** Hales returns for £75,000, becoming Charlton's most expensive player ever. **18th November 1978** Bristol Rovers 5-5 Charlton. **9th January 1979** Charlton 1-1 Maidstone United in the FA Cup third round. Flanagan and Hales are sent off in the 86th minute for fighting . . . with each other. **7th April 1979** Charlton 1-1 Preston – Andy Nelson brands fans who barracked the players "village idiots". Nelson is sacked the following March and Charlton finish bottom of the Second Division.

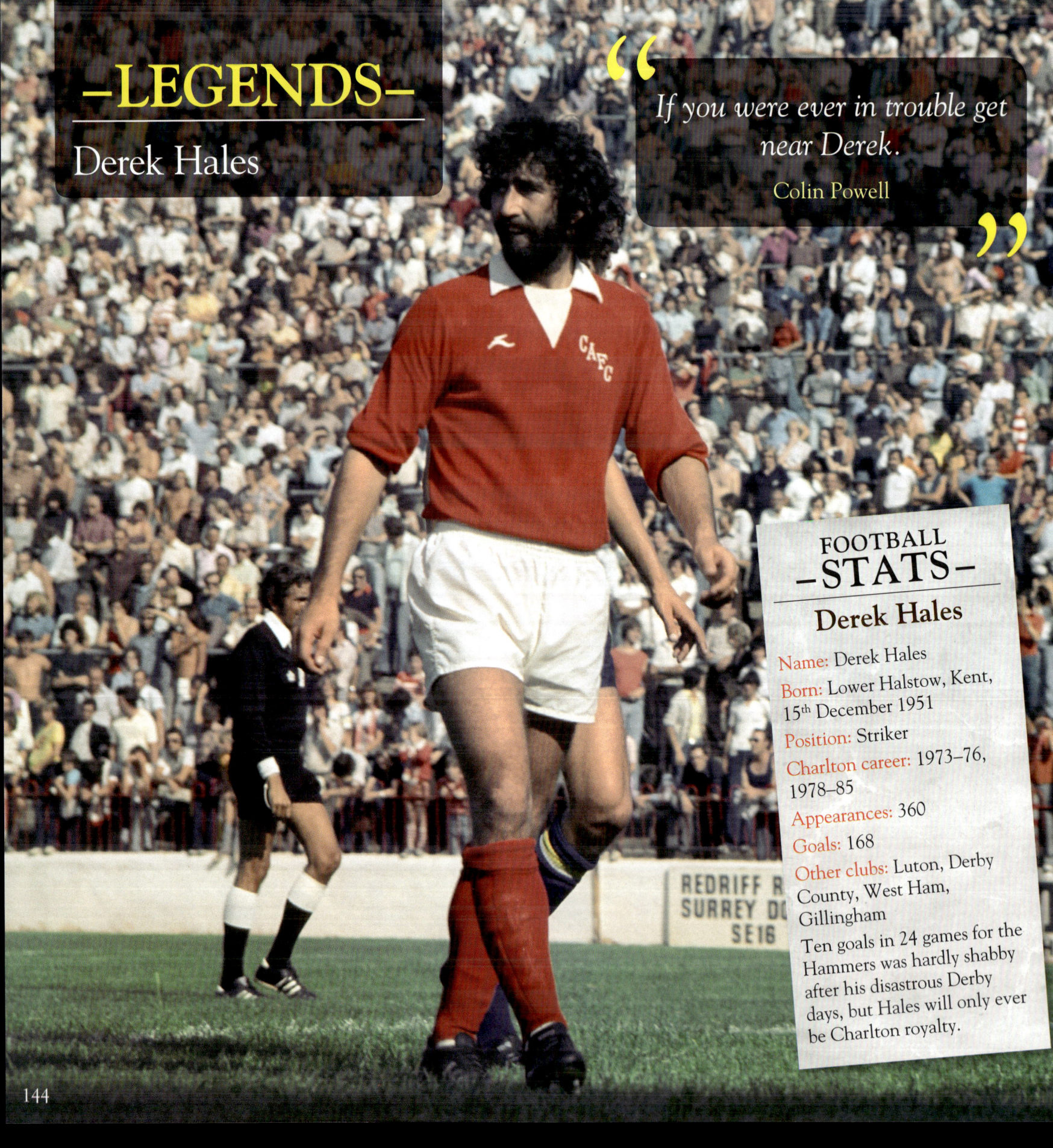

–LEGENDS–

Derek Hales

"
If you were ever in trouble get near Derek.

Colin Powell
"

FOOTBALL –STATS–

Derek Hales

Name: Derek Hales

Born: Lower Halstow, Kent, 15th December 1951

Position: Striker

Charlton career: 1973–76, 1978–85

Appearances: 360

Goals: 168

Other clubs: Luton, Derby County, West Ham, Gillingham

Ten goals in 24 games for the Hammers was hardly shabby after his disastrous Derby days, but Hales will only ever be Charlton royalty.

Hales, the King

Derek Hales wafted in from Luton for almost the same derisory fee as Charlton had paid for Johnny Summers a generation earlier. If £4,000 was cheap in 1956, then it was a robbery 17 years later for a player who would overtake Summers as Charlton's record marksman.

Hales made a scoring start in a 4-3 Third Division win over Blackburn at The Valley in September 1973, and followed up his 20 League goals in 1974–75 by bagging 28 in the next campaign.

In August 1976, the *Mirror* honoured the bearded wonder with the headline: "DUCK FOR COVER WHEN SURE-SHOT DEREK'S ABOUT!" Alongside the picture of Hales taking aim for the start of duck-shooting season, Hales told the paper: "It gives me confidence knowing I'm a marked man. It means they know what I can do – they give me respect and I like it."

The article reveals the striker had just signed a new two-year contract with Charlton "which is sure to give Second Division goalkeepers a few nightmares – not to mention the ducks."

Sadly, the ducks of Kent were able to breathe a huge sigh of relief because 'Killer' Hales was gone by Christmas, sold to First Division Derby for a big, fat profit after 16 goals in 16 games at the start of the 1976–77 season.

LEFT: Derek Hales all swash and buckle and bearded menace, especially – but not exclusively – in front of goal.

One of his last acts as a Charlton player was to whip off his kit for a tasteful photo shoot in the *Daily Mirror* studios. Here's one of the more printable 'Hotpants Hales' poses.

–LEGENDS–

Mike Flanagan

> " *I just could not see how Tottenham were overlooking his skill, strength and eye for goal. He had been on £22 a week at Spurs, and he moved to Charlton for the same . . . He went on to become a legend, as did Halesy . . . I picked up Colin Powell from Barnet. All three cost £14,000.* "
>
> Theo Foley on Flanagan

FOOTBALL –STATS–

Mike Flanagan

Name: Mike Flanagan

Born: Ilford, 9th November 1952

Position: Striker

Charlton career: 1971–79 and 1984–86

Appearances: 378

Goals: 120

Other clubs: Tottenham Hotspur, New England Tea Men, Crystal Palace, QPR, Cambridge United

In the meltdown following the Maidstone mayhem, and before being sold to Palace, 'Flash' worked as a painter and decorator with his dad's firm.

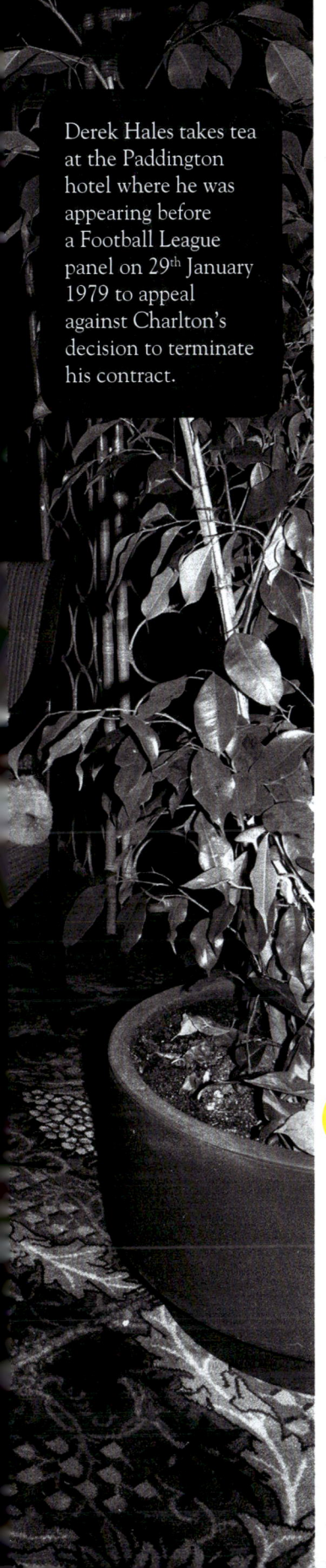

Derek Hales takes tea at the Paddington hotel where he was appearing before a Football League panel on 29th January 1979 to appeal against Charlton's decision to terminate his contract.

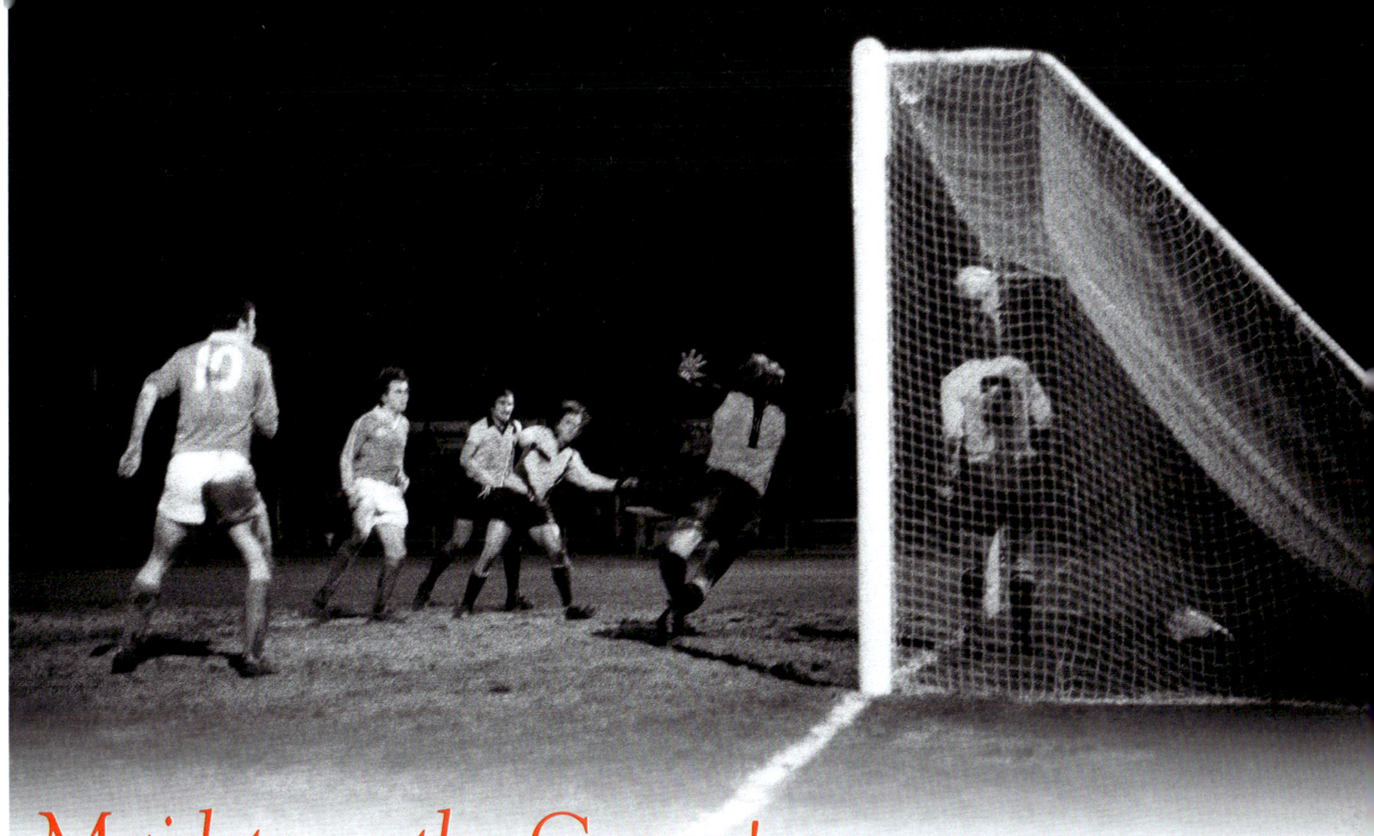

Maidstone the Crows!

FA Cup third-round replay, Maidstone United 1-2 Charlton, 15th January 1979. The decisive goal, scored by Martin Robinson with Lawrie Madden looking on, settles a tie that lives on in Addicks infamy! After his top-flight travails with Derby, who unloaded him to West Ham within nine months, Derek Hales was back at Charlton by July 1978. The incendiary Flanagan–Hales striking partnership exploded into a punch-up during the 1-1 draw with Charlton's non-League Kent neighbours at The Valley on 9th January. Both were sent off. Hales was sacked by the club who retained his registration so they could still cash in on his talents. Charlton relented and Hales was fined a fortnight's wages, while Flanagan jetted off to the Caribbean in disgust and remained an outcast until he was sold to Crystal Palace in the summer for £650,000. He, too, would be back.

> *In 20 years of refereeing I've never sent two players off from the same side for fighting each other . . . I consulted a linesman just to confirm what I had seen.*
>
> Referee Brian Martin

Mirror Sport

Telephone: (STD code 01)—353 0246
Wednesday, January 10, 1979 No. 23,305

Arsenal saved by own g

OFF! OFF!

Red card for Charlton pair in Cup war of their own . .

By TERRY SMITH
Charlton 1, Maidstone Untd 1

CHARLTON strikers Derek Hales and Mike Flanagan were sensationally sent off last night — for punching each other.

The team-mates swapped blows in a bitter mid-field flare-up after a Charlton attack had broken down five minutes from the end of this third-round FA Cup battle.

Shocked team-mates rushed to pull them part before referee Brian Martin consulted a linesman and sent both players off. Flanagan was nursing a cut under an eye.

Angry Charlton manager Andy Nelson slapped a gag on comments by his players, and said:

"I've never seen anything like this on a football pitch. The referee was right to send them off — I saw them throwing punches.

"This is the most serious happening I've had to deal with in seven years at the club. I feel so angry that if I did anything tonight I might regret it.

"We will have all the players in tomorrow and get to the bottom of it. The result doesn't matter. This serious situation over-rides the result."

Referee Martin said: "In 20 years of refereeing I've never sent two players off from the same side for fighting each other.

"I ran past them and heard one player say something to the other. I turned round and saw them exchanging blows.

"I consulted a linesman just to confirm what I had seen."

Ironically, it was the busy Flanagan who had scored Charlton's face-saving equaliser in the 77th minute.

It cancelled out Maidstone's 13th minute goal by striker Glenn Coupland, a P E teacher from Orpington.

Charlton threw everything at the Southern Leaguers in the second half, but goalkeeper Dickie Guy pulled off some great saves before he was finally beaten.

Maidstone will ask the F A to switch the replay to Tuesday because they have greyhound racing at their stadium on Monday evenings.

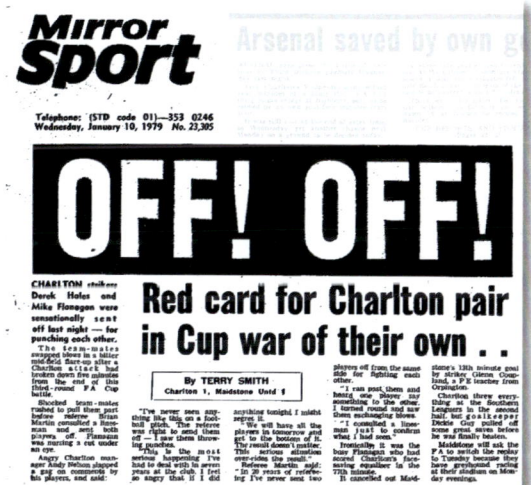

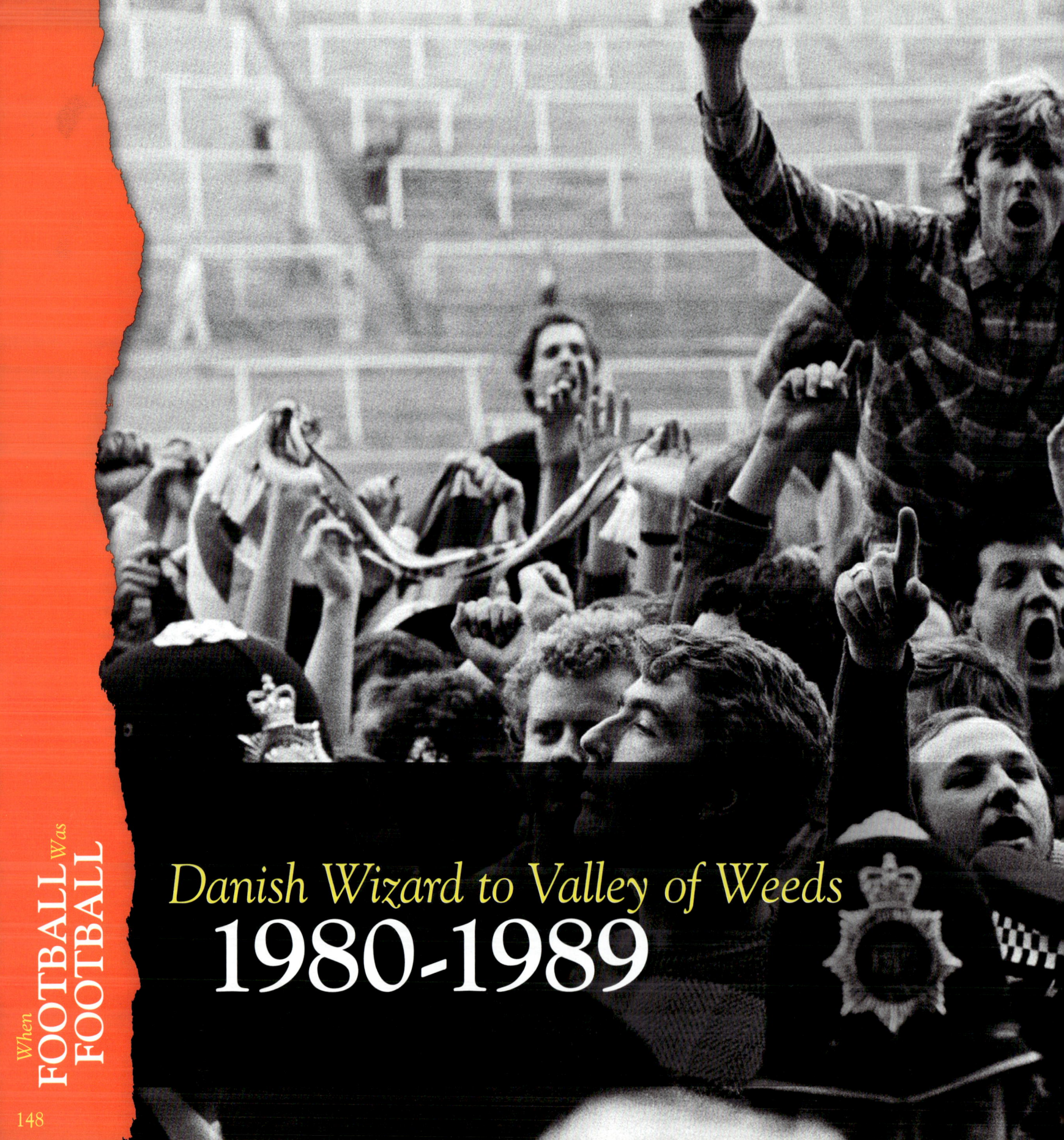

When
FOOTBALL WAS FOOTBALL

Danish Wizard to Valley of Weeds
1980-1989

> "I still can't believe Charlton will not be playing there anymore. It's tragic what is happening . . . It has virtually made me cry."
>
> Derek Hales

Charlton Athletic 2-0 Stoke City, 21st September 1985. Fans protest at The Valley's last match before the club's move to Selhurst Park.

More Downs than Ups

28th March 1980 Mike Bailey returns as manager with Charlton hurtling towards relegation to Division Three. They finish bottom. **1st November 1980** A 1-0 win at Huddersfield makes it seven straight victories – a new club record. The run extends to 15 matches unbeaten on the way to promotion. **25th April 1981** Carlisle 1-2 Charlton seals a return to the Second Division at the first attempt. **June 1981** Bailey walks out to go to Brighton while Seagulls boss Alan Mullery takes over at The Valley. **2nd June 1982** Mark Hulyer buys Charlton, ending the 50-year Gliksten rule at The Valley. Mullery is replaced by Ken Craggs, who survives less than six months. **13th November 1982** 1977 European Footballer of the Year Allan Simonsen scores after 85 minutes on his Charlton debut after signing from Barcelona. **27th November 1982** Lennie Lawrence's first match in charge is a 0-0 draw at home to Shrewsbury. **5th March 1983** Simonsen's car is vandalized after he scores twice in a 5-2 thrashing of Chelsea at The Valley.

Soap Star

Paul Walsh was one of the most exciting young forwards to come through the ranks. He was on the way up as Charlton were on their way down again. Luton got their own back for Derek Hales by pinching Walsh for £400,000. Big-money moves to Liverpool and Tottenham followed and he played five times for England.

Sheffield United 3-2 Charlton, and a booking for Derek Hales on 14th March 1981. Nothing unusual, but the kit is certainly out of the ordinary. Charlton are playing in Sheffield Wednesday shirts, rushed over to Bramall Lane from Hillsborough because of a late decision to televise the match. A TV ban on sponsors' logos meant Charlton were banned from wearing their FADS-sponsored tops.

> "You don't get to become
> European Footballer of the Year
> without being something special . . .
> I remember one game against Burnley,
> not least because I was sent off, as was
> Mark Aizlewood. We lost 7-1. Back in
> the dressing room, Lennie [Lawrence]
> wasn't very happy . . . Simonsen
> turned round and said, 'one nil, seven nil,
> it is just one defeat. Seven days later he
> scored twice in a 5-2 win against Chelsea.
>
> Derek Hales

Yes, Les, 1977 European Footballer of the Year Allan Simonsen Really is your New Charlton Team-Mate

New signing Allan Simonsen (middle), aged 29, during his first training session with the club in October 1982 before he received international clearance to play. Charlton defender Les Berry clearly cannot believe his eyes.

Magic Amid the Madness

For a brief, shining moment, one of the finest footballers on the planet wore the red and white shirt of Charlton Athletic.

Never mind that it hastened the club to the brink of doom. Or that his 16 League games produced just five wins and eight defeats, including a 7-1 battering at Burnley.

Suddenly, lining up with Terry Bullivant, Steve White and Carl Harris at Grimsby and Rotherham, was the waif-like wizard who had relegated Kevin Keegan and Michel Platini into second and third places in the 1977 Ballon D'Or. He was the only player to have scored in European Cup, UEFA Cup and European Cup Winners' Cup finals, and was a Denmark international who accumulated 55 caps.

Simonsen was said to have turned down Tottenham and Real Madrid when deemed surplus to requirements at the Nou Camp because of the arrival of another decent player – Diego Maradona.

To utter amazement, and possible concern for his mental stability, he chose Charlton. Thrusting young Addicks chairman Mark Hulyer risked everything, including £324,000 Charlton could ill afford, on a gamble that backfired spectacularly for the future of the club.

But anybody who saw Simonsen destroy Chelsea in the 5-2 League win at The Valley and almost engineer a stunning FA Cup upset against Bobby Robson's Ipswich would not begrudge a penny of it.

After 131 days, the greatest Dane was gone, with Charlton unable to meet his wages and still owing Barça around £200,000.

RIGHT: Simonsen before his debut for Charlton reserves in a Football Combination game against Swansea on 10th November 1982. More than 2,000 fans turned up to watch.

ABOVE: Simonsen in full flow.

LEFT: Ken Craggs, who replaced Alan Mullery as boss in June 1982, hugs his new superstar.

BELOW: Craggs was gone after a few months, leaving new manager Lennie Lawrence to show Simonsen some love.

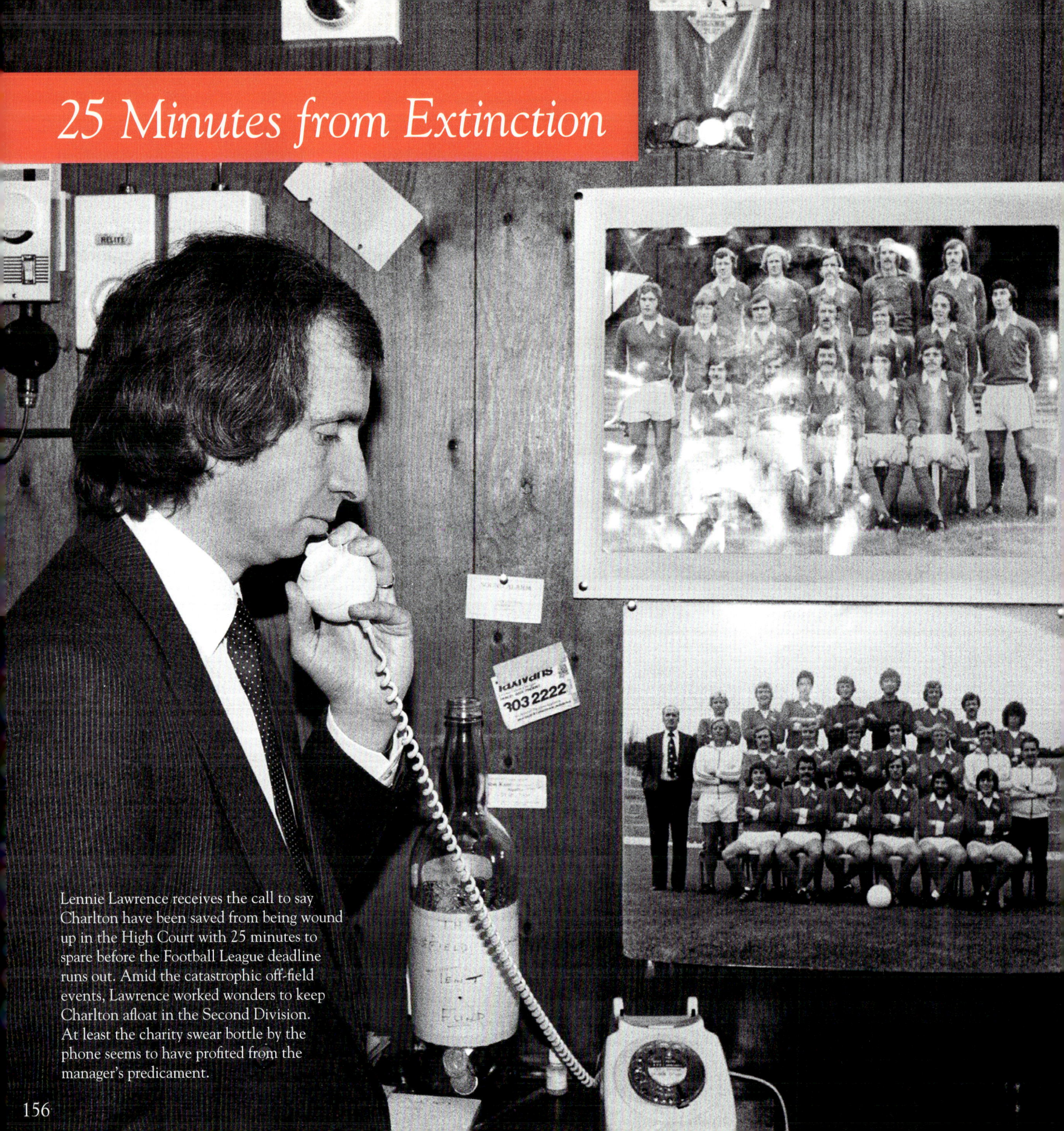

25 Minutes from Extinction

Lennie Lawrence receives the call to say Charlton have been saved from being wound up in the High Court with 25 minutes to spare before the Football League deadline runs out. Amid the catastrophic off-field events, Lawrence worked wonders to keep Charlton afloat in the Second Division. At least the charity swear bottle by the phone seems to have profited from the manager's predicament.

15th October 1983 Charlton 1-0 Manchester City – The Addicks beat one of the promotion favourites with a Derek Hales goal, while the debt collectors are closing in on Mark Hulyer who tells the *Daily Mirror*: "We haven't a hope in hell's chance of survival." **22nd October 1983** Hulyer resigns as chairman. **25th February 1984** Swansea 1-0 Charlton is widely predicted to be Charlton's last game as financial troubles threaten to sink the club. **8th March 1984** A 5.00 p.m. deadline is set by the Football League for a rescue package to be approved in the High Court. The decision goes in Charlton's favour at 4.35 p.m. **10th March 1984** John Fryer, head of the consortium that saved the club, parades with fellow directors on the pitch before the 3-3 draw with Grimsby, in which 18-year-old Robert Lee makes a goalscoring debut. **28th August 1984** Hales breaks Stuart Leary's scoring record with the first goal in a 2-2 home draw with Huddersfield. Three days earlier, he scored a hat-trick in the opening-day 3-0 win at Cardiff to draw level with the South African. **29th September 1984** Hales' 168th and final goal for Charlton in another 2-2 draw, at home to Portsmouth. In the meantime, Flanagan had returned to the club. **9th March 1985** Shrewsbury 1-1 Charlton – Hales plays his last game in front of 3,236 at Gay Meadow. **7th September 1985** Charlton 3-1 Crystal Palace – The drama of Mark Reid's three penalties, two of which he converted, passes most fans by. They are too shell-shocked from being handed a leaflet announcing the next home game, on 21st September, would be the last at The Valley.

Robert Lee scores his first Charlton goal in a 3-3 draw against Grimsby. By the end of the 1984–85 season the Addicks could not even attract 4,000 gates for games against Wolves, Middlesbrough, Cardiff and Barnsley. The Bradford City fire disaster of 11th May 1985, claimed the lives of 56 fans and was the death knell for the dilapidated Valley when the East Terrace was closed on safety grounds.

157

Angry supporters in front of the main stand on 21st September 1985. The heroes who saved Charlton Athletic in 1983 were now villains for uprooting the club. Lennie Lawrence was said to have been spat at and threatened. On the eve of the final match against Stoke, it was reported that vandals had daubed "venomous graffiti" around the ground. Slogans included: 'No sell-out', 'Charlton must not die' and the equally venom-less 'Stay at Charlton'.

BELOW: The *Daily Mirror* of 23rd September 1985, with a warning for English football.

PAGE 6   THE MIRROR, Monday, September 23, 1985

Chilling message from a heroes' graveyard

1985 Charlton 2, Stoke City 0. Division Two. Attendance, 8,858. The last goal at the Valley...Robert Lee beats Stoke's goalkeeper before yawning terraces

The cold wind from soccer Valley

1947 Charlton 3, Brentford 0, Div. One. Att. 68,000. Those were the glory days at The Valley. The great Sam Bartram is pictured above in goal.

by JOHN JACKSON

THE large sign on the condemned terracing told it all: "This Match Is Sponsored By . . ." the sponsor's name space was blank.

No-one wanted to invest in Charlton Athletic's last match at their once-majestic ground the Valley.

For the 8,858 faithful who turned up on Saturday to witness this sad slice of history in South East London it was of little consequence.

They would retain many memories of a very happy Valley, which will now almost certainly be redeveloped. As flats . . . houses . . . even offices?

BUT The Valley's last farewell was more than just an emotional moment for the handful of loyal fans.

British soccer is going bust. The decision by Charlton and Crystal Palace to share one ground seven miles away at Selhurst Park may well be prophetic.

As Ted Croker, once a Charlton player, now secretary of the Football Association, said: "This could be the beginning of a new era. If this sort of move can defray the costs for a club, then it must be good.

"Loyalty and traditions die hard. I am just sad that the games pie is my old club."

But if fans continue to stay away could there be more amalgamations of clubs now existing almost side by side?

Television personality Jimmy Hill, a Charlton director, faced mobs of angry supporters on Saturday. They wore black ties, laid wreaths on the centre spot and held a sit-in on the pitch at half-time.

And when the final whistle had blown, they took away lumps of turf for keepsakes.

Hill said: "This sort of decision is never easy, but lack of money makes it inevitable."

The fact that only 23,718 people paid to watch Charlton's four home matches this season pressed home his point.

THE Second Division club — despite a £1.5 million injection from building giants Sunley Holdings — was on the verge of bankruptcy.

And on Saturday many a ghost haunted the great East Terrace, the biggest single standing area in Europe with room for 45,000 people. But on The Valleys final day it accommodated just two stewards in bright orange jackets.

Years of neglect brought danger and a Greater London Council order for its closure.

I still remember cramming myself onto that towering terrace for a match against Arsenal in 1956 when the gates were shut after 70,000 people had clicked through the turnstiles.

Today's football climate, with its hooliganism and anti-social behaviour, would not allow such a crowd. Another factor which helped to close THE VALLEY.

Now the vast East Terrace is a monument to 66 years of soccer, lasting over 1,197 League matches.

Seventy-year-old Sailor Brown joined many old players introduced to the crowd on Saturday. He said: "I looked up at the huge terrace and I heard the roar of 70,000 throats."

And there were more tearful reminiscences, with such great names as goalkeeper Sam Bartram—later a respected columnist on the Sunday People—receiving many a mention.

EMOTION at times washed away the talk of the hard realities of soccer life.

No-one was more affected than former international player Derek Ufton, now a Charlton director.

He wrote in the programme of 'Our Valley,' and confessed: "My hand shakes and the paper is wet with my tears as the ghosts of my youth return to torment me . . ."

FOR THE RECORD: Charlton Athletic beat Stoke City 2-0 on Saturday to stay on course for possible promotion to the First Division next season.

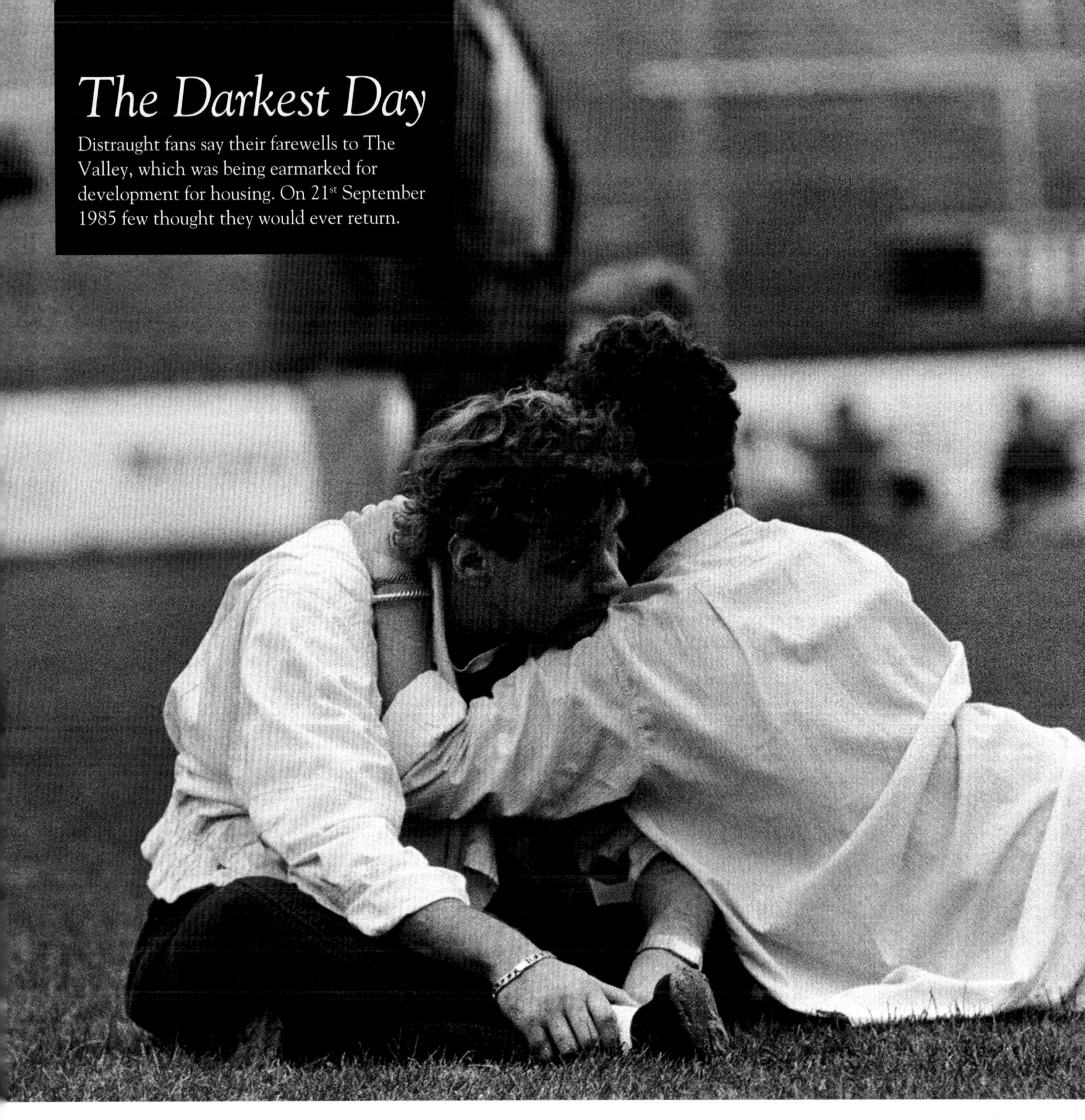

The Darkest Day

Distraught fans say their farewells to The Valley, which was being earmarked for development for housing. On 21st September 1985 few thought they would ever return.

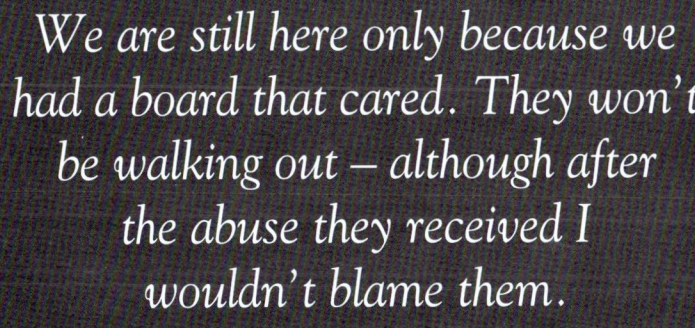

> *We are still here only because we had a board that cared. They won't be walking out – although after the abuse they received I wouldn't blame them.*
>
> Lennie Lawrence

The protests are over for now and the nets come down at the end where Robert Lee (below and left) scored the last goal. Lee – on as a 23rd-minute substitute for Mark Aizlewood – struck in the 83rd minute against the backdrop of the eerily empty East Terrace.

> "I've seen pictures of that goal so many times, giant blow-ups of it, the lot. Someone even did a painting of it. It's only when you see things like that you realize what it means to some people. But for us, as players at the time, it was just another game to be won."
>
> Robert Lee

ABOVE: Mike Flanagan on signage removal duties at The Valley.

RIGHT: Flanagan and Robert Lee are drafted in as part of the charm offensive to encourage Charlton fans to go the extra 8 miles and 70 yards to support their club at Selhurst Park.

"

I sat on the touchline as a kid when 75,000 watched the 1938 FA Cup match with Villa. My dad lifted me on to the track. I love this club – but I'd rather play at Crystal Palace than nowhere.

Derek Ufton, ex-Charlton player and a club director

"

Jim Melrose completes his hat-trick in a 3-2 win over Everton at Selhurst Park on 11th October 1986, one of the highlights of Charlton's first season back in the big time.

The Artful Lodgers

To the mixed joy and anguish of every Addicks fan, seven months on from The Valley of tears, Lennie Lawrence's Charlton finish as Second Division runners-up. But they were to play in Division One as Selhurst Park lodgers.

Palace chairman Ron Noades made conciliatory noises, declaring: "We want to be 50-50 with Charlton. We don't want either club to have the advantage over the other. There is no advantage in one club swallowing up the other. We want to work together, yet we want each club to keep its own identity and rivalry. We don't want our players mixing. Our first job is to find accommodation for them." Hence the Portakabins that would house the playing tenants for the next five years.

Lawrence's achievement ranks with that of any Charlton manager. A moribund, homeless football club, the worst-supported of almost any in the top two divisions, had risen against all the odds. He brought in two of the best full-backs in Charlton history – Mark Reid from Celtic, and John Humphrey from Wolves. Striker Jim Melrose arrived from Manchester City for £45,000 in March 1986 and his goals helped see Charlton over the promotion finishing line.

At last there was a new crop of Addicks heroes, but along with the likes of Andy Peake and Steve MacKenzie, their status as legends would be tainted by their relative or total non-acquaintance with The Valley.

Peter Shirtliff – one player from the exile years who will always be a Charlton legend.

3rd May 1986 Charlton hit back from two down to win 3-2 at Carlisle and ensure a return to the top flight after 29 years. 2,000 travelling fans chair Lennie Lawrence and chairman John Fryer around Brunton Park. **29th March 1987** Full Members Cup final – Charlton's first Wembley showpiece since the 1947 FA Cup win, ends in 1-0 defeat to Second Division Blackburn. In the first two rounds, home wins over Birmingham and Bradford are seen by a combined 1,638 souls at Selhurst Park. The 5,431 watching the semi-final against Norwich are treated to a pulsating ending. Robert Rosario puts the Canaries ahead in the 89th minute, but Colin Walsh equalizes in the first minute of injury time before an own goal by Butterworth hands Charlton victory in extra-time. **13th May 1987** FA Youth Cup final second leg, Coventry City 1-0 Charlton Athletic (aet). The Sky Blues nick it in extra-time after a 1-1 draw in the first leg at The Valley on 28th April. The Charlton team includes Carl Leaburn, Mickey Bennett, Scott Minto and Darren Pitcher.

St Andrews Day

Peter Shirtliff's goals against Leeds at St Andrews preserve Charlton's Division One status in the first year of the play-offs on 29th May 1987. The club finishing just above the relegation places had to square-off in a two-legged knockout involving the third-, fourth- and fifth-placed clubs in Division Two. Charlton won their semi-final 2-1 against Ipswich. The final goes to a replay after the sides are tied at 1-1. For the second leg, Colin Walsh recalls being welcomed to Elland Road by one Leeds nutter repeatedly head-butting the Charlton team bus. Just 3,000 or so Selhurst-fatigued fans made the trip to Birmingham where Charlton skipper Shirtliff stunned the 17,000-strong Leeds army with his barnstorming late double, as the Addicks roared back from a goal down in extra-time.

LEFT ABOVE: Shirtliff fires in the equalizer.

LEFT: 'Captain Fantastic' – Shirtliff after his play-off heroics.

Shirtliff's bullet header makes it 2-1. The two Leeds men closest to Shirtliff and failing to stop him burying the winner are John Pearson and former Charlton captain Mark Aizlewood, who had both left the Addicks for Elland Road that season.

Arsenal 2-2 Charlton, 21st March 1989. Paul Mortimer with Carl Leaburn, Paul Williams and Mark Reid, after putting the Addicks one up at Highbury. A 14th-place finish marks Charlton's best season back in the First Division.

Ex-Newcastle and Arsenal star Malcolm Macdonald, a *Mirror* columnist at the time, among the triffids at The Valley in September 1987.

Voice of the Valley NO 1 FEB 88 30p
The only INDEPENDENT Charlton mag

MESSAGE TO OUR SUPPORTERS

CHARLTON ATHLETIC

On March 26....

LET'S GO HOME

ABSOLUTELY NO CONNECTION WITH CASC OR CAFC

Charlton were just about holding their own in the First Division, but they were never going to be a force while scraping by on crowds averaging less than 8,700 at Selhurst Park. In February 1988, disenfranchised supporters found a new voice in the fight to restore Charlton to their true home – the *Voice of the Valley*, a fanzine prepared to challenge all those barring the way to a return to London SE7.

"
There are weeds three feet high where once Derek Hales claimed goalscoring records. The goalmouths are choked with greenery . . . . the nails driven into the doors of rusting turnstiles might as well be driven into supporters' hearts.

Voice of the Valley, issue one, February 1988
"

Back to The Valley
1989-1992

> " *I had no idea of the depth of feeling among supporters who wanted Charlton back at The Valley.*
>
> Charlton chairman Roger Alwen "

Like all your Christmases coming at once . . . The Valley homecoming of 5th December 1992.

23rd March 1989 Official announcement that Charlton Athletic will once again play football at The Valley. However, there's many a slip . . .

2nd April 1989 Addicks fans flock to the derelict, weed-strewn Valley in answer to the club's appeal for help in clearing up. **January 1990** Greenwich Council rejects planning application to rebuild The Valley. **3rd May 1990** The fans' Valley Party fields 60 candidates in council elections, polling almost 15,000 votes and unseating the planning chairman in local elections. Away from the ballot box, Charlton finish 13 points adrift of safety and are relegated with Millwall. **24th October 1990** Charlton supporters' club charter a Boeing 737 to take 130 fans to Newcastle where the Addicks win 3-1. **April 1991** A new Valley planning proposal is passed by Greenwich Council.

4th May 1991 Charlton 1-1 West Ham – Scott Minto scores the last goal after five years and 225 days at Selhurst Park. But with The Valley still a tip, Charlton shift their digs across the Thames to Upton Park. **July 1991** Lennie Lawrence resigns after nine years. Alan Curbishley and Steve Gritt are put in charge as joint player-coaches.

18th January 1992 Newcastle 3-4 Charlton – Alan Pardew's 89th-minute strike seals another of those comebacks Charlton specialize in, this time from 3-0 down.

Addicks fans flock to the derelict Valley in answer to the club's appeal for help in clearing three-and-a-half years of rot and neglect, 2nd April 1989. The anticipated two-week operation took two hours. As a bonfire blazes, volunteers enjoy a kickabout on The Valley turnip field. They might not have been quite so happy if they had known Charlton would not kick a ball in anger there for another three years and eight months. After a planning refusal in January 1990, chairman Roger Alwen tells the *Mirror*: "I can't see Charlton ever going back to The Valley. It's very sad because it would be a dream crushed."

175

> *I loved my time at Charlton despite all the trials and tribulations . . . I'd experienced more in nine years than most managers do in their whole careers.*
>
> Lennie Lawrence

BELOW: Curbs playing at Manchester City in November 1986. Five years later he was part of another Charlton first when he and Steve Gritt were made joint player-coaches.

> *For me, The Valley will always be Charlton. It was the terraces I used to sweep there and this is where the heart of the club will always be.*
>
> Billy Bonds

Two years on from the great centre-circle burn-up, the dream is back on, 4th April 1991. There is much work still to be done inside and outside the ramshackle ground before these boys' heroes finally run out again to 'When the Red, Red Robin'.

> *The management were keen that we went to the ground before the day and got used to the pitch and the surroundings. We trained there on both the Thursday and Friday to get a feel of the place, and then we played on the Saturday.*
>
> Charlton captain Simon Webster

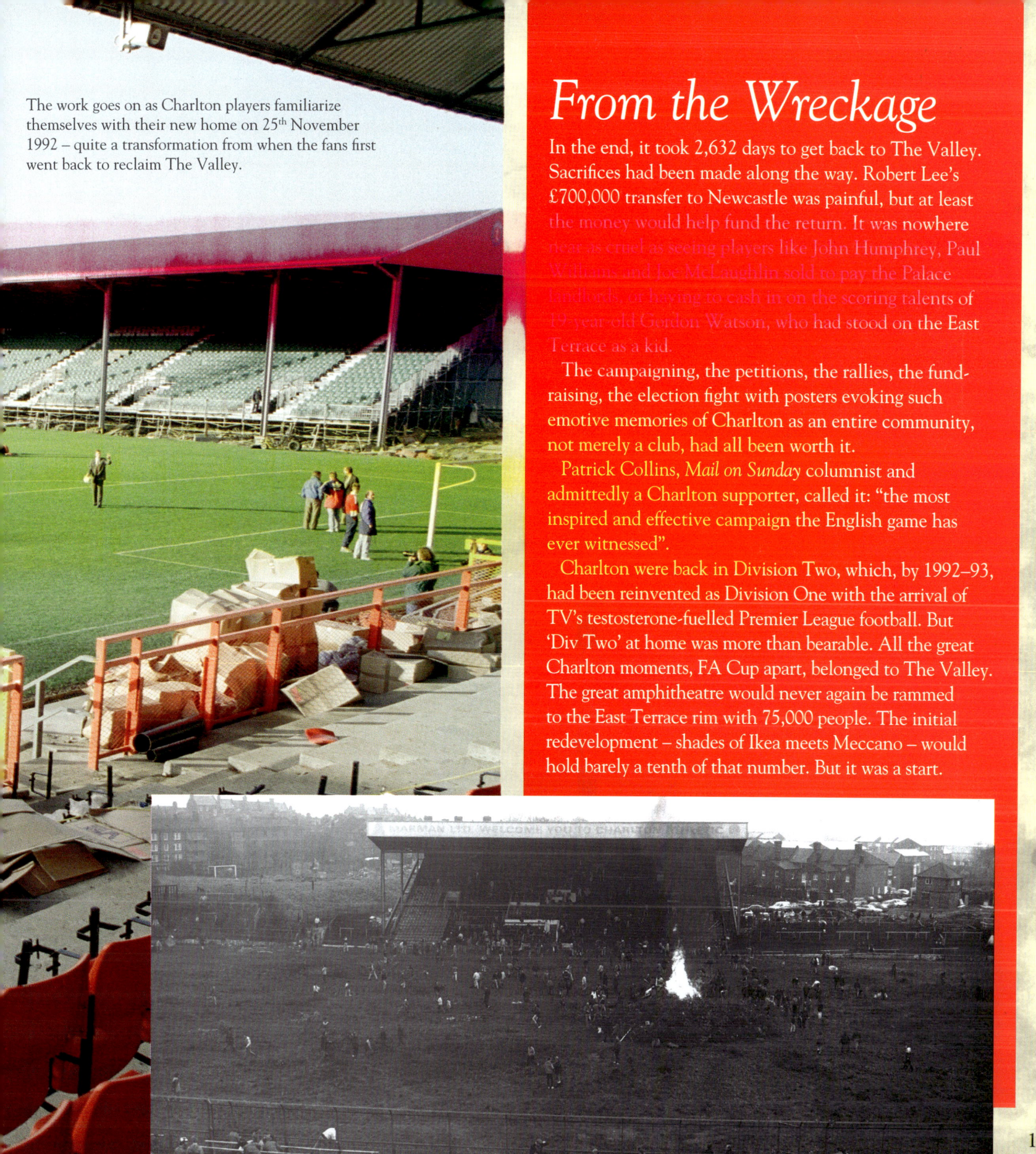

The work goes on as Charlton players familiarize themselves with their new home on 25th November 1992 – quite a transformation from when the fans first went back to reclaim The Valley.

From the Wreckage

In the end, it took 2,632 days to get back to The Valley. Sacrifices had been made along the way. Robert Lee's £700,000 transfer to Newcastle was painful, but at least the money would help fund the return. It was nowhere near as cruel as seeing players like John Humphrey, Paul Williams and Joe McLaughlin sold to pay the Palace landlords, or having to cash in on the scoring talents of 19-year old Gordon Watson, who had stood on the East Terrace as a kid.

The campaigning, the petitions, the rallies, the fund-raising, the election fight with posters evoking such emotive memories of Charlton as an entire community, not merely a club, had all been worth it.

Patrick Collins, *Mail on Sunday* columnist and admittedly a Charlton supporter, called it: "the most inspired and effective campaign the English game has ever witnessed".

Charlton were back in Division Two, which, by 1992–93, had been reinvented as Division One with the arrival of TV's testosterone-fuelled Premier League football. But 'Div Two' at home was more than bearable. All the great Charlton moments, FA Cup apart, belonged to The Valley. The great amphitheatre would never again be rammed to the East Terrace rim with 75,000 people. The initial redevelopment – shades of Ikea meets Meccano – would hold barely a tenth of that number. But it was a start.

LEFT: Charlton 1-3 Newcastle – Garry Nelson chases down John Beresford in the last match at Upton Park on 14th November 1992. The switch from Selhurst Park was intended to be for just three matches, but it turned into a season and a half. However, after seven years, the Addicks really were heading home.

RIGHT: Joint player-coaches Curbishley and Gritt doff hardhats at the rebuilt Valley.

Happy Valley Returns

The homecoming. Many fans had already been back, of course – to mourn; to peer through the rusted railings in Floyd Road at a football graveyard; to squeeze through gaps or clamber over the old turnstiles and survey the ruins. Even in the old paying, playing days, bunking in for nothing was a rite of passage for many a young Addick.

In the programme for the Newcastle match on 14th November, Charlton's last as squatters at West Ham, the police had a message for the supporters: "I hope you will enhance your reputation on your return. If you have a ticket please arrive at the ground early. It will take time to become accustomed to the new entrances to each stand and find your seat. If you arrive at the ground just before kick-off you will miss the start – the match will not be delayed. If you have not been lucky enough to get a ticket please keep away from the area."

Chairman Roger Alwen cast his mind back those seven-odd years, recalling how fans had hurled their scarves away in the centre circle in a final gesture of sorrow and anger on 21st September 1985: "We'll make sure there are some scarves out there before the match, so supporters can come and reclaim them. It's a new beginning."

Joint player-coach Steve Gritt admitted: "I'm frightened, apprehensive. I'm not sleeping at night and I've got butterflies in my stomach. The players mustn't let down all the people who have believed in Charlton. I hope whoever has written the script has got the ending right."

Tarmac was still being laid on the morning of the match. Construction crews had been buzzing around till late the previous evening and hardhats were still in evidence hours before the kick-off against Portsmouth.

Co-boss Alan Curbishley meant business, concerned after four straight defeats and a run of just four points from the last 30. But he, too, appreciated the significance of the occasion, saying: "This is our home now. Not Selhurst Park or Upton Park. Charlton belong to The Valley. We are back home."

But this was a day for the supporters – just 8,700 of them because of safety considerations, with the East Terrace still starkly empty. None would forget it.

FAR RIGHT: Painting the town red . . . fans lucky enough to get tickets for the first match back at The Valley.

183

A parade of Charlton legends on 5th December 1992 – to great acclaim compared to their understandably more muted reception in 1985, when their appearance and a 'special souvenir programme' were less appreciated amid the gloom of leaving The Valley.

185

SPORTS Mirror

HAPPY

GREAT TO BE BACK: Colin Walsh's winning goal is cause for colourful celebration on Charlton's Valley return   Pictures: DALE CHERRY

VALLEY

£2million welcome home for Charlton

By PHIL STILES

THE GLORY days came back to London SE7 as Charlton made a highly emotional return to the Valley after a seven year absence – and celebrated with a thrilling victory over Portsmouth.

Colin Walsh's seventh minute goal sparked huge celebrations amongst the sell out 8,337 crowd and joint player-manager Alan Curbishley said: "At last we're a club again, instead of being just part of a club.

"This could be the turning point of our season. The crowd were magnificent and I haven't heard a roar like the one we had today for seven years.

Before the game, Charlton received a £2million cheque from Football League president Gordon McKeag – the Football Trust's contribution towards a project which has so far cost £1.5million.

March

After 360 'home' matches played at Selhurst Park and Upton Park, Charlton's never-say-die fans had raised £1.1million themselves to ensure an historic homecoming.

More than 1,000 fans marched from Woolwich Town Hall to the Valley in celebration and balloons, bands and a parade of former star players turned the day into a carnival.

Fellow boss Steve Gritt, who made his first start of the season and received the Man of the Match award into the bargain, said: "I was very tired but I was carried along on a wave of adrenalin. The supporters deserved this day."

The match had been sold out for two weeks – some were climbing trees to get a slice of the action yesterday – and the tickets for the next three home games have all gone.

Chairman Roger Alwen bubbled: "We were still laying tarmac at 11am, but everything worked perfectly."

Even Portsmouth manager Jim Smith had to admit: "I think the atmosphere got to some of my players – but I'm glad that Charlton are back where they belong."

FAN-TASTIC: Garry Nelson applauds the Valley crowd

WE'RE BACK – PAGE 41

9 770956 807015

Serial No. 1,447 ©MGN Ltd. 1992

FOOTBALL
–STATS–

Colin Walsh

Name: Colin Walsh

Born: Hamilton, 22nd July 1962

Position: Midfielder

Charlton career: 1986–96

Appearances: 269

Goals: 30

Other clubs: Nottingham Forest, Peterborough, Middlesbrough

Arguably the finest left peg in football – broken at Newcastle in November 1987 and again soon after his return – crowned an incredible Valley homecoming.

Colin Walsh high-fives Darren Pitcher after scoring the only goal as Charlton celebrate their Valley return by beating Portsmouth, 5th December 1992. Walsh also hit the post twice, but the *Mirror* named Steve Gritt, the only one in the line-up to have played at The Valley before, as man of the match. The full Charlton team was: Bob Bolder, Darren Pitcher, Scott Minto, Steve Gritt, Simon Webster, Stuart Balmer, John Robinson, Lee Power, Carl Leaburn, Garry Nelson, Colin Walsh. The subs were Kim Grant and Alan Pardew.

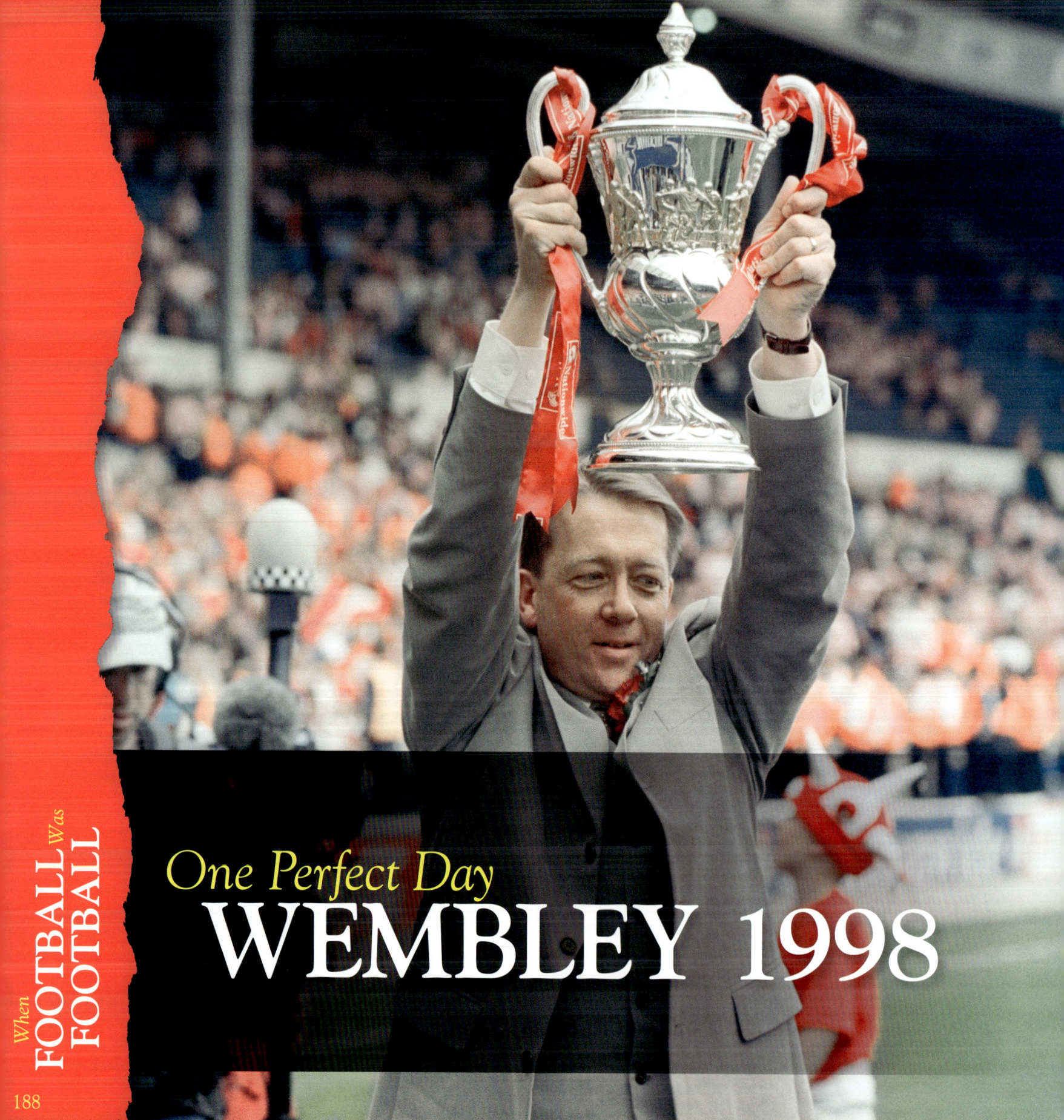

One Perfect Day
WEMBLEY 1998

LEFT: Alan Curbishley lifts the Division One play-off final trophy, Bank Holiday Monday, 25th May 1998.

> "
> *We had a slight problem deciding who would take the sixth penalty, and then the seventh. I left it to the lads and they sorted it out.*
>
> Alan Curbishley
> "

RIGHT: Wembley hat-trick hero Clive Mendonca.

Prem, here we come! Shootout hero Saša Ilić leads the partying
– the Aussie-Serb goalie had been playing for Dr Martens League
side St Leonards FC six months earlier.

Clive Mendonca scores the first of his three goals – the most famous Wembley hat-trick since Geoff Hurst's in 1966.

If Leeds at St Andrews was *Saving Private Ryan*, then Sunderland at Wembley in 1998 was *Gone With the Wind*, *Citizen Kane* and *The Magnificent Seven* all rolled into one for heart-thumping play-off drama. Mendonca's brilliant hat-trick, Richard Rufus' stunning first-ever goal, 3-3 after 90 minutes, 4-4 after extra-time, Saša Ilić saving Michael Gray's daisy-cutter and Charlton winning 7-6 on penalties. It was Neverland stuff in the year before the wrecking balls and bulldozers rolled in to flatten English football's home of legends. And it was achieved by Alan Curbishley with a bunch of players who had cost just £1.7 million. A day that lives in the hearts of at least 33,000 of the 77,739 who were there.

> *Seeing as I hadn't saved anything all day, it was really only right that I saved one of the penalties.*
>
> Saša Ilić

RIGHT: Steve Jones gets carried away after Richard Rufus makes it 3-3 with five minutes of normal time remaining.

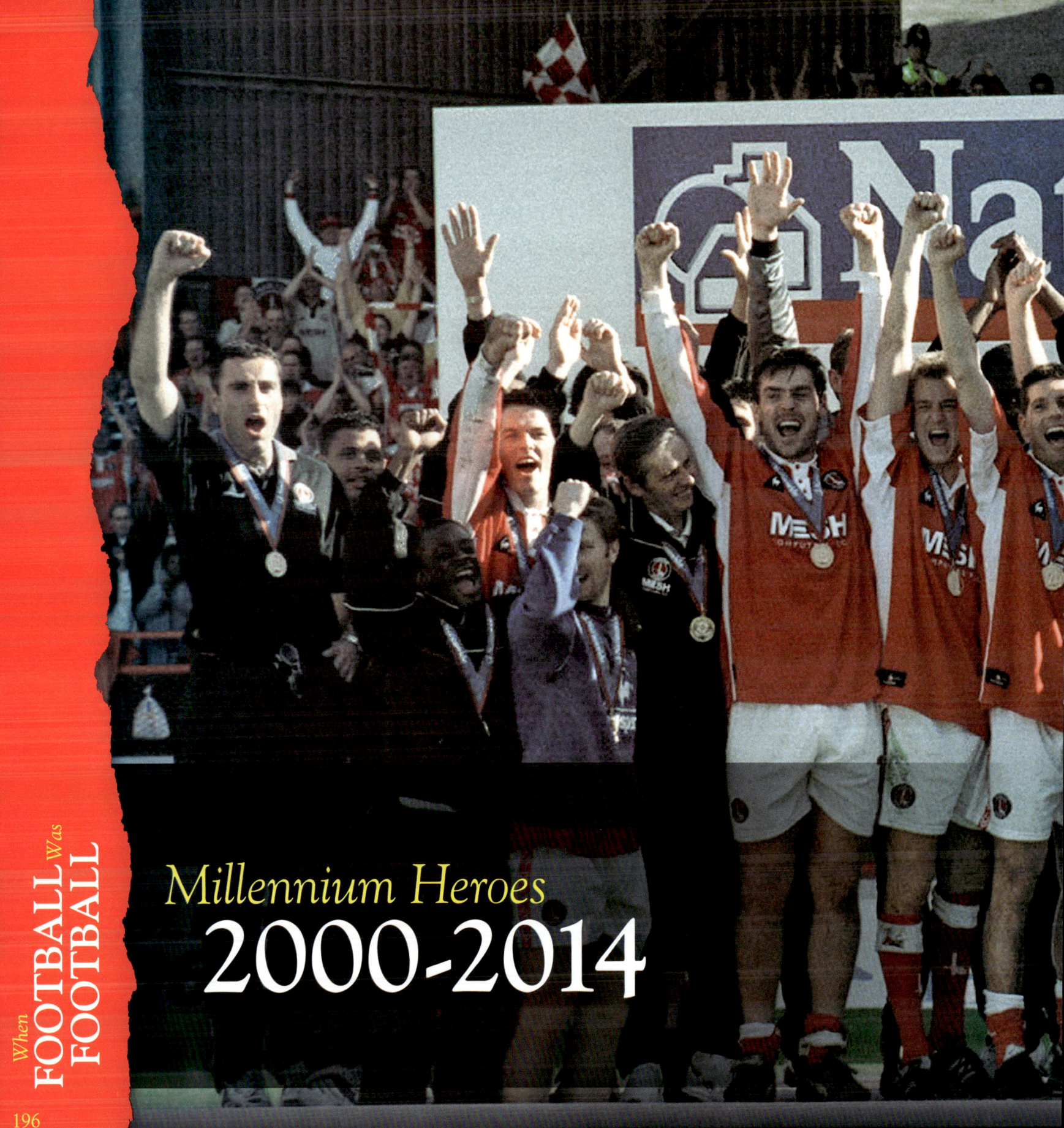

Millennium Heroes

2000-2014

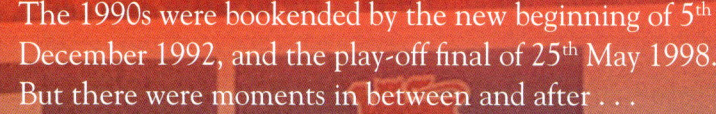

The 1990s were bookended by the new beginning of 5th December 1992, and the play-off final of 25th May 1998. But there were moments in between and after . . .

"

It's 36 years since Charlton had an English international, and it's me. My name's been put up on the honours board in the reception. I look at it and I can't believe it's my name.

Charlton's Chris Powell, after his England debut on 28th February 2001

"

Charlton are crowned Football League Division One Champions at The Valley and return to the Premier League on 29th April 2000. Even a 3-1 defeat to Ipswich could not spoil the party.

12th October 1993 Brescia 2-0 Charlton – Charlton's first competitive game in Europe in the Anglo-Italian Cup. **8th February 1994** Blackburn 0-1 Charlton – Kenny Dalglish's Shearer-era moneybags Rovers are beaten by a 15th-minute Darren Pitcher goal in the FA Cup third-round replay. **12th March 1994** Man United 3-1 Charlton – Charlton's first FA Cup quarter-final since 1947, with 10,500 Addicks fans making the trip to Old Trafford. **15th June 1995** Steve Gritt is sacked after 18 years at Charlton, leaving Curbishley in sole charge. **Summer 1999** Charlton sign a co-operation deal with Italian giants Inter Milan, prompting hope that some of Brazil star Ronaldo's mates could end up on exchange deals at The Valley. **19th February 2000** Bolton 1-0 Charlton – A second FA Cup quarter-final in six years, with 5,601 fans watching the game beamed back to The Valley. **24th April 2000** Relegated after only a season in the top flight, Charlton bounce straight back and become First Division Champions with 1-1 draw at Blackburn.

–LEGENDS–

Mark Kinsella

FOOTBALL
–STATS–

Mark Kinsella

Name: Mark Kinsella

Born: Dublin, 12th August 1972

Position: Midfielder

Charlton career: 1996–2002

Appearances: 218

Goals: 23

Other clubs: Home Farm, Colchester, Aston Villa, West Bromwich Albion, Walsall

It's amazing what £150,000 could buy back then. Charlton were slow to sign him from Colchester and too quick to take Villa's £750,000 for the inspirational Addicks engine driver and captain.

–LEGENDS–

John Robinson

FOOTBALL –STATS–

John Robinson

Name: John Robinson

Born: Bulawayo, Zimbabwe, 29th August 1971

Position: Midfielder

Charlton career: 1992–2003

Appearances: 338

Goals: 44

Other clubs: Brighton, Cardiff, Gillingham, Crawley

Robinson was a cheap replacement for Robert Lee and, according to Curbs, "played as much a part in the rise of Charlton in the last 10 years as anybody."

ABOVE: Feisty Robbo could start an argument in a confessional.

-LEGENDS-

Chris Powell

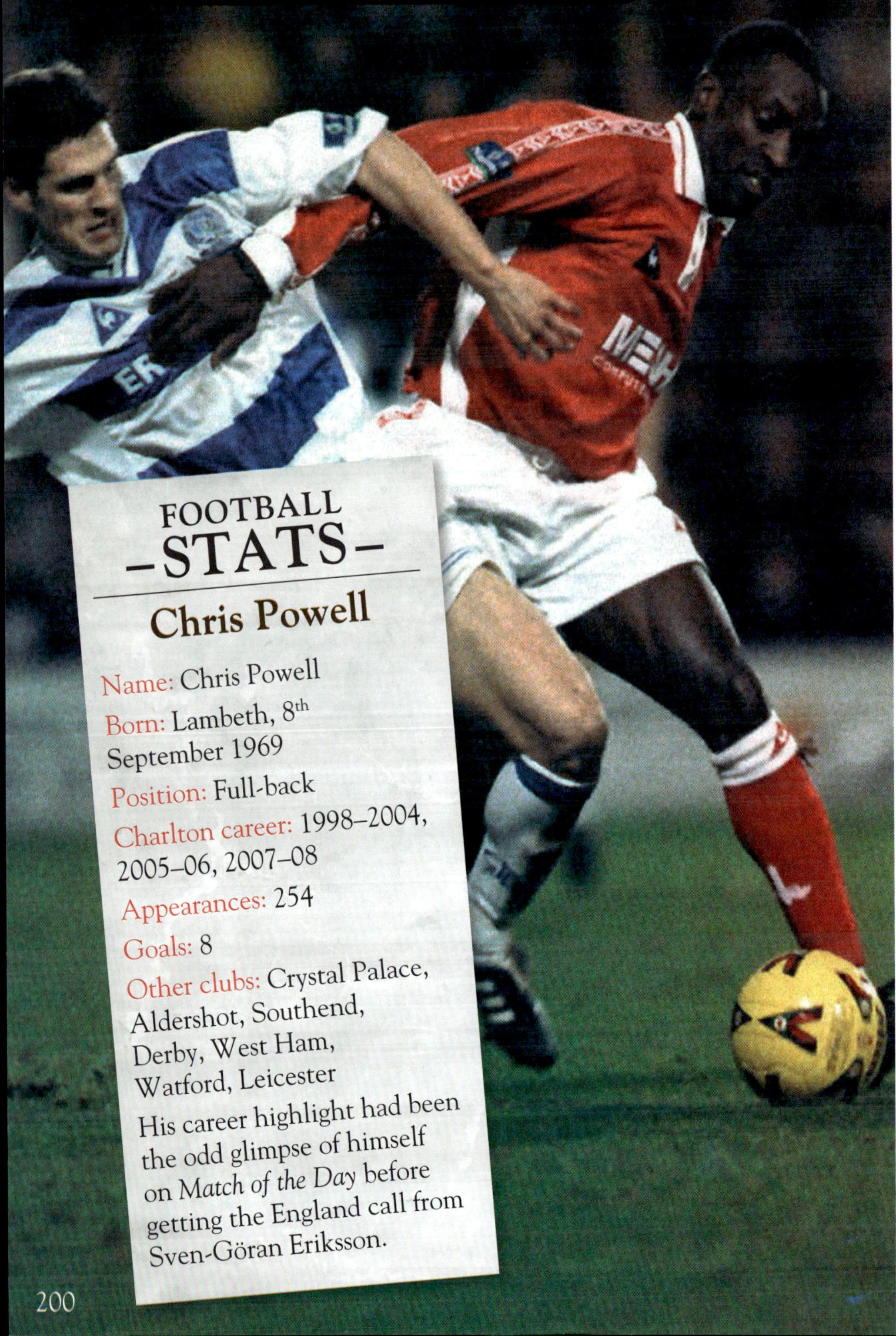

FOOTBALL
-STATS-

Chris Powell

Name: Chris Powell

Born: Lambeth, 8th September 1969

Position: Full-back

Charlton career: 1998–2004, 2005–06, 2007–08

Appearances: 254

Goals: 8

Other clubs: Crystal Palace, Aldershot, Southend, Derby, West Ham, Watford, Leicester

His career highlight had been the odd glimpse of himself on *Match of the Day* before getting the England call from Sven-Göran Eriksson.

-LEGENDS-

Richard Rufus

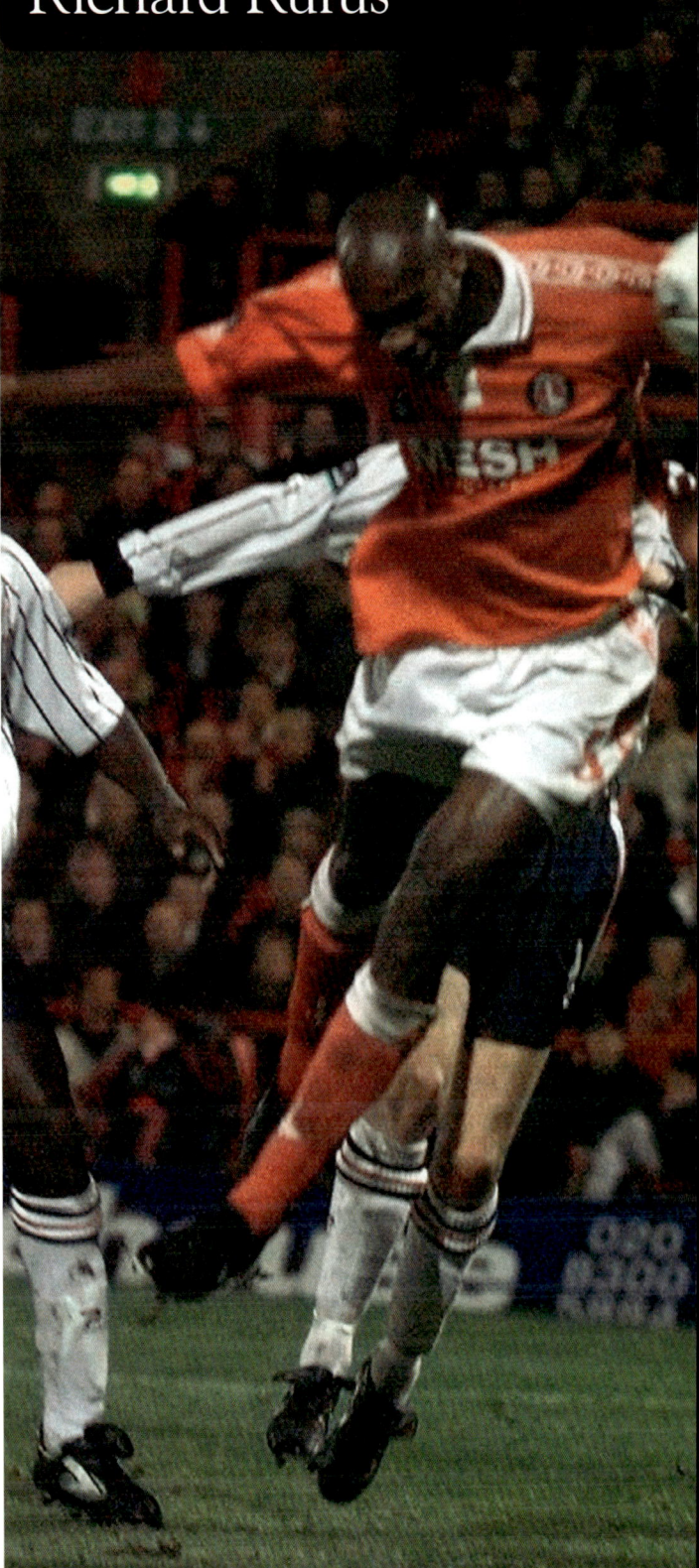

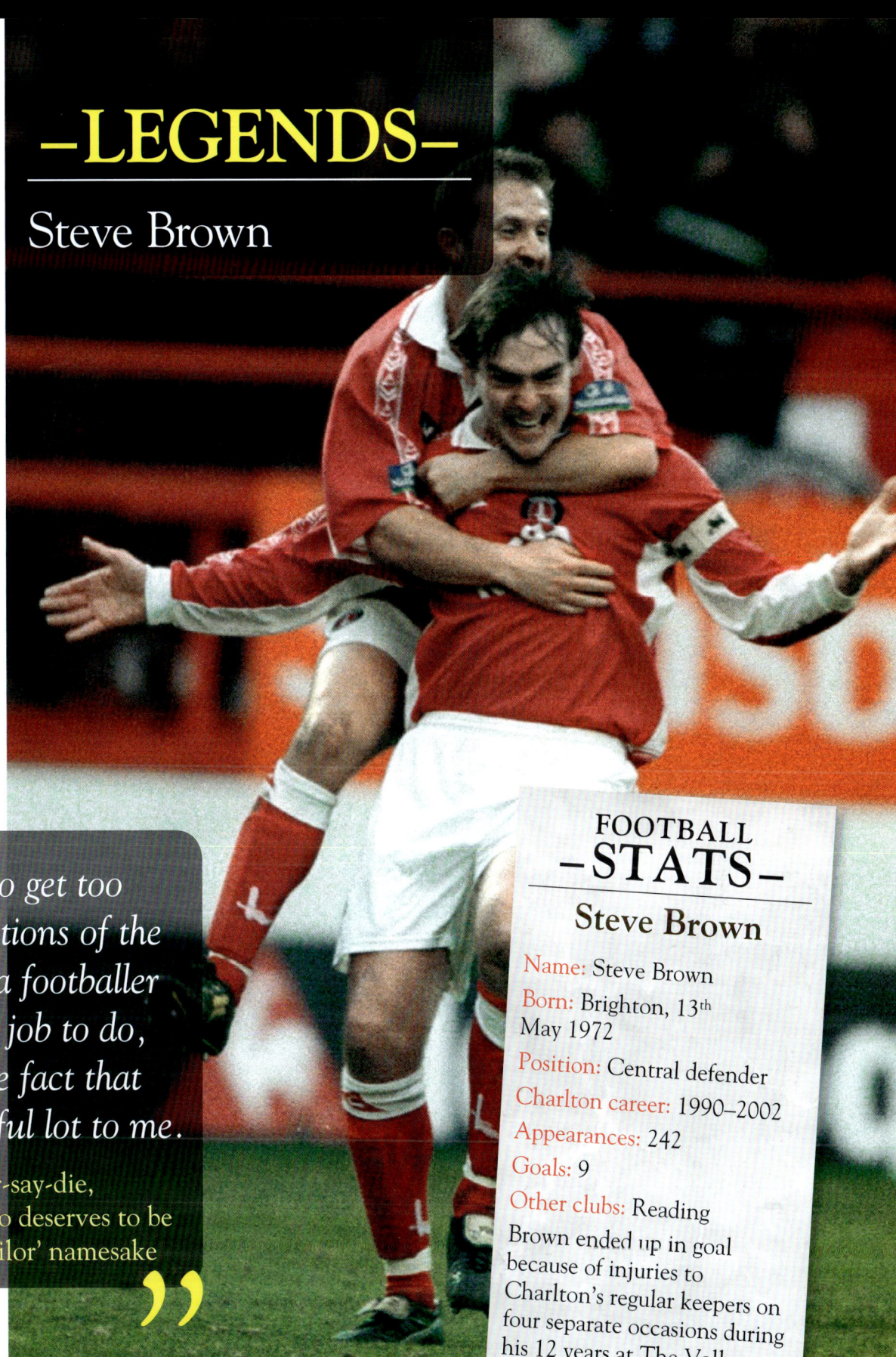

FOOTBALL –STATS–

Richard Rufus

Name: Richard Rufus

Born: Lewisham, 12th January 1975

Position: Central defender

Charlton career: 1993–2004

Appearances: 322

Goals: 14

Other clubs: None

His career was ended by knee problems but he was a colossus at the back . . . and up front after his Wembley play-off goal.

Steve Brown

"

You're not meant to get too involved with the emotions of the whole thing if you're a footballer because you've got a job to do, but I can't ignore the fact that Charlton means an awful lot to me.

Steve Brown – a never-say-die, thunder-thighed defender who deserves to be treasured as dearly as his 'Sailor' namesake

"

FOOTBALL –STATS–

Steve Brown

Name: Steve Brown

Born: Brighton, 13th May 1972

Position: Central defender

Charlton career: 1990–2002

Appearances: 242

Goals: 9

Other clubs: Reading

Brown ended up in goal because of injuries to Charlton's regular keepers on four separate occasions during his 12 years at The Valley.

January 2004 Scott Parker is sold to Chelsea for £10 million. **9th June 2005** Charlton legends parade at The Valley again for the club's 100th anniversary and for the Sam Bartram statue unveiling. **14th November 2006** From having one of the longest-serving bosses in football, Charlton dispense with Iain Dowie less than six months after he replaced Alan Curbishley. Les Reed, former FA technical director, who has never managed a football club, takes over. **24th December 2006** Reed is sacked after seven games and 40 days, the shortest reign in Premier League history. Alan Pardew gets the job. **7th May 2007** Charlton Athletic 0-2 Tottenham – Charlton are relegated after seven seasons in the top flight. **22nd November 2008** Charlton lose 5-2 to Sheffield United at home, slip into the Championship relegation zone and Pardew is sacked. A worst-ever run of 18 games without a win sees the Addicks finish bottom. **5th September 2009** A record start to a season as Charlton beat Brentford 2-0 at The Valley for their sixth successive win in League One. **4th January 2011** Phil Parkinson is sacked as boss after a 4-2 home defeat to Swindon with Charlton fifth in League One. **22nd January 2011** Charlton 2-0 Plymouth – Chris Powell's first game as manager and a first win since November. **21st April 2012** Charlton 2-1 Wycombe – Charlton are League One Champions with a club record points total of 101.

Strife after Curbs

ABOVE: Iain Dowie, a week before he was canned, and Pardew (below).

–LEGENDS–

Dean Kiely

FOOTBALL –STATS–

Dean Kiely

Name: Dean Kiely

Born: Salford, 10th October 1970

Position: Goalkeeper

Charlton career: 1999–2006

Appearances: 248

Other clubs: Coventry, Ipswich, York, Bury, Portsmouth, Luton, West Bromwich Albion

Kiely won just 11 Ireland caps, as Shay Given hogged the jersey. When Mick McCarthy had his infamous World Cup bust-up with Roy Keane, Deano put himself forward as a 'midfield dynamo' to try to get a game!

Clive Mendonca

Charlton waited a long time for another Charlie Vaughan, Johnny Summers or Derek Hales. Clive Mendonca was that priceless striker, arriving for £725,000 from Grimsby and scoring 28 goals in his first season – crowned, of course, by the Wembley hat-trick. His treble in the first home match of the 1998–99 campaign put Charlton at the summit of English football's top flight for the first time since 1937. Unfortunately he was plagued by back problems and forced to retire in 2002.

FOOTBALL –STATS–

Clive Mendonca

Name: Clive Mendonca

Born: Sunderland, 9th September 1968

Position: Striker

Charlton career: 1997–2002

Appearances: 91

Goals: 48

Other clubs: Sheffield United, Doncaster, Rotherham, Grimsby

Mendonca received death threats after beating hometown club Sunderland in the play-off final and sold the hat-trick match ball and his medals at auction in January 2012.

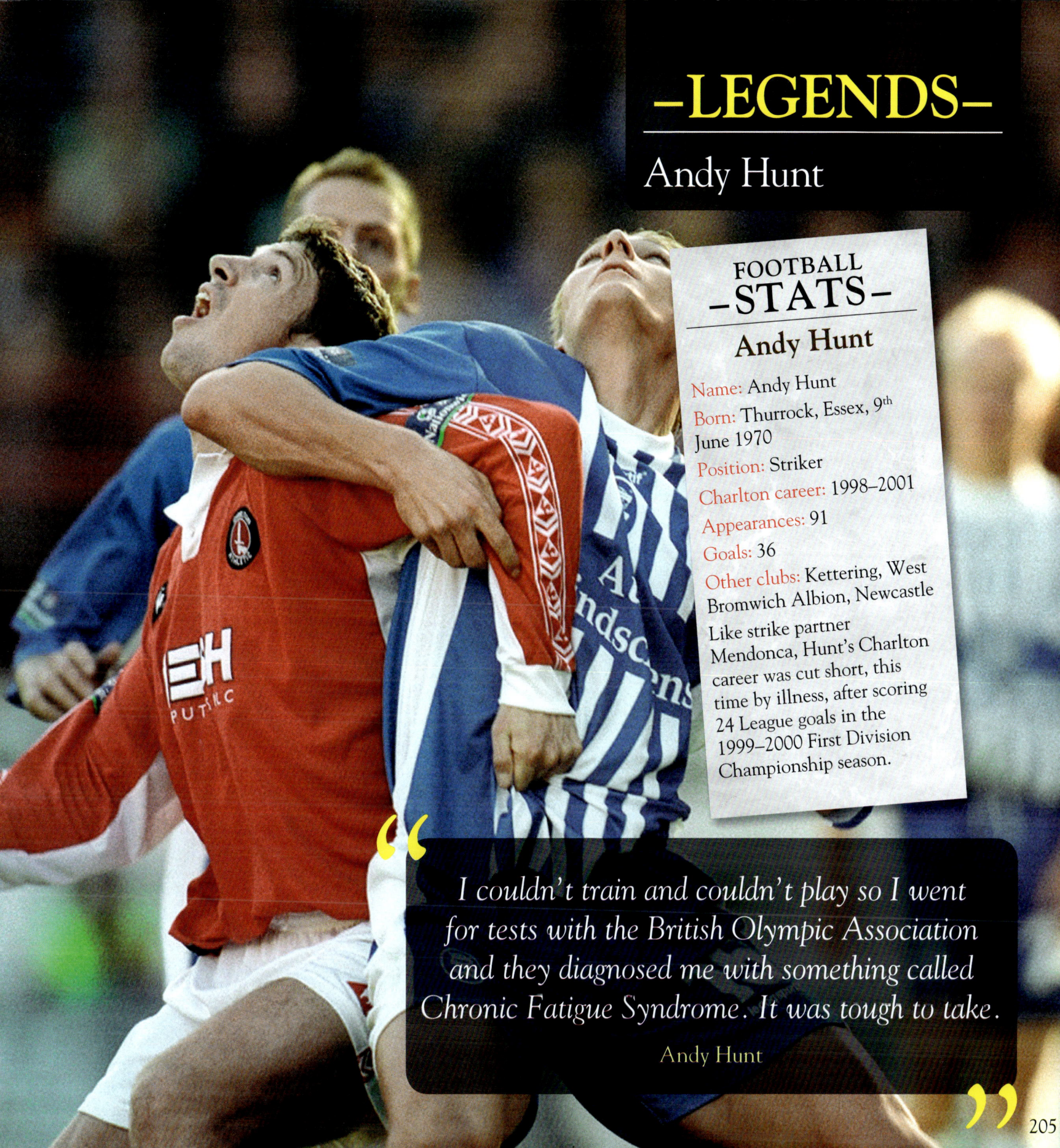

–LEGENDS–

Andy Hunt

FOOTBALL –STATS–

Andy Hunt

Name: Andy Hunt
Born: Thurrock, Essex, 9th June 1970
Position: Striker
Charlton career: 1998–2001
Appearances: 91
Goals: 36
Other clubs: Kettering, West Bromwich Albion, Newcastle

Like strike partner Mendonca, Hunt's Charlton career was cut short, this time by illness, after scoring 24 League goals in the 1999–2000 First Division Championship season.

"
I couldn't train and couldn't play so I went for tests with the British Olympic Association and they diagnosed me with something called Chronic Fatigue Syndrome. It was tough to take.

Andy Hunt
"

The Eternal Flame

By the end of 2013, Charlton fans won the right for The Valley to be listed as an Asset of Community Value – providing protection against the ground being sold off and perhaps preventing the possibility of another seven years in the wilderness.

2014 brought a new owner when Belgian entrepreneur Roland Duchâtelet paid a reported £14 million to buy the club. Well, we always dreamed of a European adventure!

Young fans lift the pre-floodlights gloom as Charlton beat Burton Albion 7-0 in the third round of the FA Cup on 7th January 1956. The torch now passes to another generation . . . six-year-old George How is pictured on his first trip to The Valley, 29th December 2013.

Acknowledgements

Thanks to the 'When Football Was Football' team – Fergus McKenna, David Scripps, Simon Flavin and Vito Inglese of Mirrorpix, and Richard Havers, Kevin Gardner and Elizabeth Stone for Haynes Publishing. I am especially grateful to Keith Peacock for perfectly setting the scene for our mazy dribble through the ages.
Thanks also to Iain Liddle at Charlton Athletic Football Club.

This is a nostalgic kick-around in the *Daily Mirror* vaults rather than a history lesson, but credit must go to those chroniclers of all things 'Addick' – Richard Redden and the late Colin Cameron, and to unsung authors of 50 years of Charlton programmes in the bottom of my wardrobe.

I'd like to dedicate this book to Julie, Bethany, Kathleen, Poppy, George, Harry, Megan and James. If they cannot all share my obsession, then maybe Sam, Eddie, Killer, Keith, Simo and Co will help them to understand it.